'Andy Lamberton has done
wonderfully imaginative me
life as a contemporary and r
As younger Christians in post-Christendom come to terms with our new situation within what some have called "the empire of desire", and seek to live faithfully within it as "foreigners and exiles" (1 Peter 2:11), this book will prove to be an important resource. I warmly commend it!'

Iain Provan: Marshall Sheppard Professor of Biblical Studies, Regent College

'The essence of anyone's faith journey with Jesus is a dynamic, daring and devoted relationship; it's a call to discipleship. *Letters for Exiles* provides anyone seeking to fulfil the costly call of being a follower of the risen Christ with the confidence to keep persevering, keep fighting the good fight and to keep focused. Through these wonderfully imaginative letters written by Abel, who is just a few steps ahead in the journey of life, Daniel is being encouraged to grasp the full reality of what it means to be a faithful follower. In turn, Andy reminds us to acknowledge the exile we live in, of the importance of journeying alongside other like-minded disciples, and that we follow the champion and perfector of our faith...now that is exciting!'

Damian Wharton: General Director, Scripture Union Northern Ireland

'I was sitting around a table almost a decade ago when I first heard Andy Lamberton use the metaphor of the Babylonian exile to describe the context in which the next generation would carry faith. It felt insightful and possible then, but it is both prophetic and real now. At that table Andy mused about who it might have been who mentored Daniel to prepare him to live out his faith in God in the way he did. Those musings have morphed into writings, as Andy has crafted this masterpiece to imagine letters written by an older, wiser and faithful friend to a young disciple navigating the fresh challenges of Babylon. This book is dripping in rich biblical narrative and strengthened by the context in which Andy himself has lived his life. He understands from personal experience what it means to live for God in environments where you might be standing alone, and he has dedicated years of his life to being a mentor to a generation of young disciples, helping prepare them for that very scenario. Andy is the real deal, and this book both captures his calling and expresses his heart. Read it for yourself, but also put multiple copies into the hands of young disciples to help prepare them for Babylon.'

Rick Hill: Secretary for Council for Mission in Ireland with the Presbyterian Church, and author of Deep Roots of Resilient Disciples

'It comes as no surprise that this book follows the rhythm of the character of the author: authentic, disciple-making, missional and Bible-honouring. Andy is the real deal and anything he says regarding discipleship is worth listening to. I encourage you to read this book slowly and prayerfully, taking time to doodle, write, reflect and allow the Holy Spirit to speak through it.'

Mitch: Evangelist, Crown Jesus Ministries

Letters for Exiles

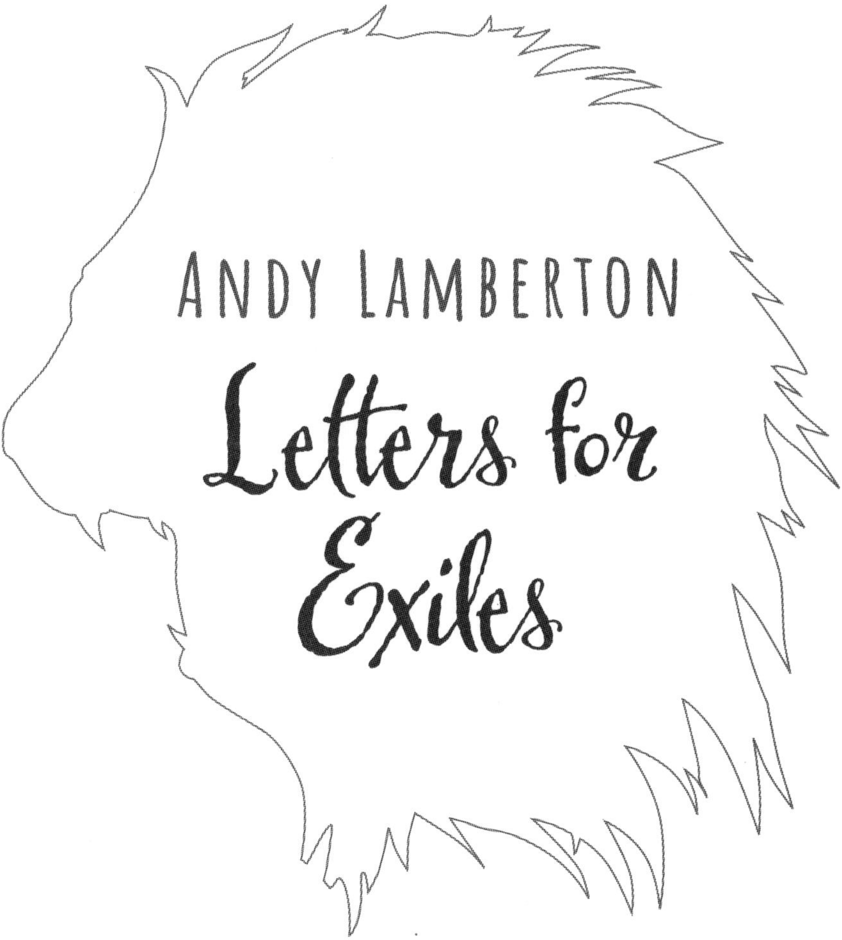

ANDY LAMBERTON

Letters for Exiles

FAITHFUL LIVING IN A FAITHLESS WORLD

10 Publishing
a division of 10 of those.com

First published in Great Britain in 2023

British Library Cataloguing in Publication Data
A record for this book is available from the British Library

ISBN: 9781914966453

Designed by Jude May
Cover images © Grandfailure | iStock, © Vector Tradition | Adobe Stock

Printed in Denmark
10Publishing, a division of 10ofthose.com
Unit C, Tomlinson Road, Leyland, PR25 2DY, England
Email: info@10ofthose.com
Website: www.10ofthose.com

1 3 5 7 10 8 6 4 2

To my children, Peter, Sarah, Matthew and Hannah,

'Don't let anyone look down on you because you are young, but set an example for the believers in speech, in conduct, in love, in faith and in purity' (1 Timothy 4:12).

I pray you will enjoy following Jesus as much as I have, and more. He is always worth it, always better and always there. He will lead; you only need to follow.

I am a rich man because you are my children, and I love you,

Dad.

Also to Adam and Jack,

'... continue in what you have learned and become convinced of' (2 Timothy 3:14).

Contents

FOREWORD

This book is a gift! It is for such a time as this. Andy has written a fresh, creative and intriguing insight into 'living in a strange land'. There is so much here for mind, body and soul. It is God-honouring, faith-building and life-inspiring.

Although set in the time of Daniel's exile in Babylon several thousand years ago, the wisdom revealed is life-transforming for twenty-first-century followers of Jesus. Vitally important principles are shared in the letters of a mentor to a mentee, Abel to Daniel. Nothing has changed in God's call to His people to be a holy people.

In another part of the Old Testament God said, 'my servant Caleb has a different spirit and follows me wholeheartedly' (Numbers 14:24). Abel, the older encourager, prayerfully and practically supports Daniel, the younger believer, who is in exile in a secular culture and country. They are two people seeking to live with that different spirit and follow their God wholeheartedly ... just like Caleb did.

Andy clearly shows practical ways twenty-first-century disciples can meet the stretching challenges of living in a culture that is increasingly permeated by practices and principles which are not God-focused. In a striking way, he skilfully paints a beautiful picture of how we work out Peter's call to live really good and godly lives as foreigners and exiles in an alien culture (1 Peter 2:11–13).

There is such a freshness in some of Andy's phrases:

- 'Time passed like a darting rabbit ...'
- 'It would be to surf the splash rather than the tide.'
- 'Invite Him, not your ego, to sit on the throne of your heart.'
- 'God has created you for much more than monotonous living.'
- '... the wisdom of wrinkles ...'
- 'It's not a giving up but a giving over.'

I have loved reading this book, and I warmly and joyfully commend it. There is so much to learn and to be shared with others. Andy's writings have the potential to be a channel of blessing in many lives. This sentence, in many ways, sums up the vision of the book: 'Be who God envisioned when He made you, when He rescued you and when He set you in the mix of this new culture, where you can live whole and bright among the broken darkness.'

Let's heed the call to live the life and be people with a different spirit! This book will certainly help us walk the trail of being the surrendered people God has called us to be!

Bishop Ken Fanta Clarke

Preface

Judah has gone into exile.
She dwells among the nations.

(Lamentations 1:3)

There is no Netflix show on the practice of being godly. Developing virtue or Christlikeness does not grab the attention of our time. I fear they're not even concepts we think about, never mind lifestyles we practise. And we're in exile. Yes, *exile*. We're following Jesus through an unwelcoming country, yet a country we love and call home.

I grew up as a farmer, on the Donegal shoreline in the Republic of Ireland. Raised by Christian parents, I am now raising my own children in what is the least evangelised English-speaking area in the world.

I came to faith when I was 14. Both then and now I want to live: to claw out all the distraction and muck in my life and run unshackled with Jesus; to give salvation its space; to breathe in the fullness our Saviour promised. But my surroundings are not helpful: I'm squeezed in with bored people distracted by their own success. I want running mates, or even a church where there are enough of us that I can hear others sing.

In my early years as a disciple, I would hop across the border, into Northern Ireland (one of the most evangelised areas in the world), to find someone to sing with, to find running mates. I learned to articulate my faith in that different environment, my discipleship shaped by people who were not outnumbered. But how do I follow Christ in this place I call home and yet still feels alien to my faith? And as most Western Christians are ushered into exile by a secularising society, I am convinced we *all* must learn to thrive here in this foreign land. How do we negotiate these times and stay true to Christ? How do we live free in exile?

And so began my calling into vocational ministry: to contribute to the body of Christ in raising up a generation ready for the exile – prepared to be godly in a foreign land. Over these years I've seen amazing young people rise up and take a stand, contributing to genuine mission and living holy lives in an unwholesome culture. Their witness for Christ echoes what we see displayed by Daniel and his friends. That great mix of skill and faith; dependence and gumption; allowing what we believe to decide how we act. Even more striking is the faithfulness of God. For I have seen the fourth friend with these modern-day exiles as they have faced their blazing furnaces. I have seen the boldness in their conviction, the compassion in their prayers and the consistency of their faith, as the One who tames lions guides them into life in all its fullness.

This book is written not only with them in mind but also their mentors: the few who invest in a few but make a world of difference.

Introduction

There are certain moments throughout history where one particular Bible story or another carry profound significance and shed light on the road ahead for God's people. The right text for the right time. As our western society becomes increasingly secular, I believe Daniel's story is such a story for today.

In Daniel 1 we read of Jerusalem besieged then conquered by the Babylonians. Daniel, along with many other promising young men, was taken into exile to be trained in the ways of his captors. Despite all the temptations and pressures, Daniel stays true to the God of Israel and lives a life of remarkable significance. His faith is steady, his engagement with Babylon high-achieving, his discernment motivating. Yet Daniel was young when he was taken, mid to late teens, most likely. So, as I allow the story of Daniel to marinate in my imagination I have to ask: who inspired Daniel's wisdom and tenacity, which we so desperately need in the church today? Who discipled Daniel? How was Daniel prepared to live for God's Kingdom in a foreign land?

Perhaps he had a mentor growing up who continued to instruct him in those early days of exile?

The idea of a mature believer equipping Daniel took hold of me and has grown into this book of letters. To start, I created a fictional character called Abel, who would act as Daniel's mentor. Here's the premise: Abel was a bondservant to Daniel's family and became Daniel's tutor. When Daniel is taken by the Babylonians, Abel decides to write letters for Daniel so he can learn to live free while in exile, to be godly in a foreign land.

I tried to write these letters as true as I could, not thinking of us today so much, but asking what would discipleship look like at this point of history in the ancient world. Abel's letters draw from the teaching of Jeremiah, Israel's prophet at that time, and other key Old Testament passages and stories.

But I bet you're asking: why would I read a bunch of old made-up letters? It is my hope Abel's letters act like triggers in your mind, helping to spark your imagination towards how you can live for Jesus today. This is not a book about 'try harder' or 'be better'. Rather it's about a perspective shift. As a fellow follower of Jesus, I want to help you face the questions we all have as we become increasingly surrounded by a secular culture. The times they are a changing, but Jesus' offer of life in all its fullness remains. And I believe, with my whole being, that we can not only face this incoming tide but see it for what it is, and embrace a higher call to live free, with Jesus as our King, the Bible as our compass, prayer as our guide and God's presence as our home.

There are three sections, each followed by a 'Time to Discuss' which includes some discussion questions and suggested Bible reading. You can do this on your own but you'll gain so much more if you read the book with a friend, a small group or an older Christian. I recommend that you agree to meet four times to discuss and pray. Once, as you begin this journey together, and then at the end of each section, where you'll find the questions to discuss.

Before you start, here are my top tips for reading this book:

- Watch the Bible Project's video: 'The Way of the Exile'. You'll find it at bibleproject.com/explore/video/the-way-of-the-exile/
- Download a Bible app, stick in your headphones, go for a walk and listen to Daniel chapters 1–6 in one go. It'll take just over half an hour and you'll get 3,400 steps in!
- Read with a pen or highlighter in your hand and a Bible by your side. This book should look messy when you're finished!

Daniel could have easily despaired when the Babylonians led him into exile, but he stood firm, trusting his God. The story captures me. And that fascination has led me to share these letters with you now. But as we start this journey let's not forget that it is Daniel's God, not Daniel, who made the difference and moved the nations like pawns. And it is the same God who has placed me here and you where you are. And it is He who will guide us to be salt and light through the uncharted waters of a post-truth, secularising world.

So the question is, are you ready? Are you ready to follow Jesus into exile and live free on this godly adventure, serving the higher throne?

To think about:

1. Do you think Daniel's experience is similar to the conditions in which we live as Christians today? How or how not?
2. If you are reading this with a friend, small group or older Christian: How can you get the most out of this book and your times together?

One wise person went up against a city
of warriors
and brought down the stronghold in which
they trusted.

(Proverbs 21:22, NRSV*)*

Dear Daniel,

You're gone. And I cannot believe it. The future looks different for all of us, and our world will never be the same again. We were warned of this, but it is so final now, so eternal. Some things I do know though. You are on the cusp of adventure: the world is still your gift and God is still your guide. I have confidence, knowing the God of Abraham, Isaac and Jacob is also God over Babylon. And I have little doubt that God's grace will guide you. His love and goodness will follow you even in this hour.

I'm planning to write you a series of letters over these coming days. I'll make arrangements to send them to you – through Mishael, probably. I do not know how much I will get to write – is there any hope for an old servant like me during these times? Educated, yes; potential, no. I'm at peace should I be lost in this invasion. You, however, who are young and of noble birth, have been given the opportunity of exile.

My understanding is the Babylonians are not like the historical occupying forces we read about during your schooling. They seek to re-educate, to rebrand the people they capture, tuning them to sing the Babylonian anthem. There is a sophistication in their brutality – it's not just power but a comprehensive vision that sets them apart. Yet while they have access to the information of the nations, it does not make them wise; while they have sciences, astronomy and sorcery, it does not make them right; while King Nebuchadnezzar has power, he does not sit on *the* throne.

I will write these letters to keep you company, and to give you some helpful perspectives and instruction as you enter this new beginning. I say this in hope, knowing at any moment my life could be over. But if I achieve anything in my final days, it'll be this.

My dear Daniel, may the rhythms of worshipful living make you feel so alive, so focused and so bright in a city so dead, so distracted and so dark. Though Babylon will change you, I pray that you will change Babylon all the more as you soar with the God of Jacob, inspiring integrity, bringing peace and pointing towards the King of Kings.

Keep your eyes open,

Abel

SECTION ONE

Questions I Think You Will Be Asking

Nebuchadnezzar king of Babylon has devoured us,
he has thrown us into confusion.
(Jeremiah 51:34)

1

In Whose Story Am I?

If you, Israel, will return,
then return to me.

(Jeremiah 4:1)

Dear Daniel,

It would seem God is not fatigued in telling stories. His imagination must be endless, revealing a new chapter with each one of us. The story He is telling with our lives, in this exile, is beyond my creative capacity, but not God's. When we read the history books of our nation, we see He has a mastery of storytelling in which every aspect of our lives – even the hurt – can somehow be part of His grand narrative. It is both global and local, present-day and across the centuries; it involves you there and me here. And the invite still stands: to participate from His side; to be part of His kingdom; to live free from the fear that the story might end badly.

we must live by faith in the Storyteller. Yet what l have in the end when we can look back over these years and see God's guiding hand over us.

So let's think about that end for a moment. Say you reach 80 years. Imagine yourself as 'old man Daniel', writing out the story of your life: what do you want him to write? How do you want him to describe his first year in Babylon? What regrets do you hope he doesn't have?

I am not suggesting you can determine the plot of your life. You can, however, decide what kind of man you want to be. How will you respond to threat? Where will you show generosity? Will you be someone who takes responsibility or someone who shies away from engagement in Babylonian society?

Will you be selfish or kind?

Godly or diluted?

Decisive or ambivalent?

Prayerful or ignorant?

Consistent with your values or changeable of heart?

*

I may have a history of telling you what to do – one you've outgrown – but I am going to take a few liberties of influence over these letters. I will make suggestions I trust will help you navigate the story God wants to tell with your life.

This, dear Daniel, is one of them: when you get to Babylon, rise early the next morning – before dawn – to prayerfully reflect. Imagine yourself, in 70 years' time, looking back over a life lived for God. Ask yourself: what kind of a man you would want to remember? What would be the contents of his character and convictions?

You have the opportunity to start again, so before you know what your opportunities are, work out what kind of man you want to be. Allow that to define you. Then, as opportunities come, you can embrace them with a knowing confidence in who you are, and in whose story you are a part.

If you don't think about who you want to be, Babylon will do that for you. You will take a seat in *their* discipleship course and begin the gradual deconstruction of your faith. Your relationship with God will be reduced to a thought you once had and placed on a shelf in your memory's bookcase, alongside the other chapters of your so-called life experiences. You will end up claiming God only in heritage and lose your distinctiveness as a follower of the One True King. Like ink that's dried up, no longer of use to the writer of a story, the dried-up disciple is of no use to God.

So let's open our eyes, remember our calling; let's play our part in the plot of God's story.

Daniel, when our father Abraham looked into the heavens and saw the constellations pulsing like waves in the giant ocean of stars, one of those stars was alight for you. When God promised him descendants who would bless the world, he had you in mind. Your life is beyond meaningful; it is divinely purposed. Your life, my life, Mishael's life: each of us is one of those stars contributing to the great project of lighting up the darkness. You are part of what God is doing.

So take your place, and shine.

*

Imagine coming to the end of your life and realising you've lived the wrong story. What a great sadness it would be to exist as a story untold, to have potential but never try. Do not make this your tale. For we are God's people, invited to be part of a story with eternal significance. Yet we can short-change ourselves by forgetting two basic truths: that God is the Author of this story, and that He invites us to play a unique role.

God is the Author of this story

God is not *our* creation and this is not *our* story. *He* is the Author of our days. Our God is not part of us or something we have constructed to make sense of the world. He is wholly other. We have not made an image to worship – it's the other way round: He made us in *His* image and calls us to worship Him. We are not inviting God into *our* lives – it's the other way round: He invites us into *His* vision for the future and beckons us to follow. This perspective is the foundation for answering your current question – 'In whose story am I?'

You play a unique role

There has never been a you before – not from the dawn of time – and there will never be anyone like you again. God created you, not someone else, for this time and in this place. He created you within your family and with your acquaintances, your opportunities, your challenges and your skillset. You have an original God-scripted adventure to live. And Daniel, what a setting you have in which to be godly, so take it. Take the opportunity to engage and be part of the Babylonian society, but not as a puppet. Be who God created you to be. Be the Daniel your older self would be proud of, the Daniel heaven sees.

Who knows what God may achieve in the story of your life – never mind the story of the exile; never mind the ageless story the Ancient of Days is telling across all of history. And you, Daniel, are included in God's story. Even the smallest of your acts is entwined in this grand narrative. The name you hold, the friends you make, the way you pray, the manner you address people, even the food you eat will be part of this tale.

Keep your eyes open,

Abel

To think about:

1. Imagine you are 80 years old, looking back at your life. How would you like to describe yourself from now to then? Use some of Abel's questions for Daniel, near the start of the letter, to get you thinking.
2. Spend some time in prayer thinking through the 'two basic truths', which are as true for you as they were for Daniel. Acknowledge God as the Author of your story, and accept His commission for you to play a unique role.
3. Will you rise early tomorrow to pray and think about the kind of person you are going to be?

2

Am I Strong Enough?

If you stumble in safe country,
how will you manage in the thickets …?
(Jeremiah 12:5)

Dear Daniel,

Today marks a month since you were taken and I can all but hold the quill. The city is quiet, dead quiet. My chest is tight, as if buckled by a belt, allowing only the narrowest of breath. Fear has set in.

Throughout the invasion I have mostly felt the sense of duty, or even love. But tonight I am scared. My mind knows to not let it control my actions, so I have sat to write. However, I dread that if I do not acknowledge the fear, I will be unable to write with honesty.

One sound I do hear – your father. He is in the main house grieving, moving from sorrow to anger and back. Joseph and I are the only servants left. All have gone, or are hiding. It's approaching dawn now and I doubt our invaders will continue their pillage until midday. What has happened to us is deep and I do not feel strong enough.

O Daniel, just now as I try to write this line, the sun is beginning to rise again.

The fear has not gone, but my chest is easing.

Breathe. His mercy is new each morning. Even this morning.

Breathe again.

It is easy when things are going well to mindlessly allow life to pass by. And yet I wonder if God gives times of ease so we can bank a storehouse of spiritual riches and rhythms to help us endure – or dare I say to thrive – in such times as we are in now. We will remember in the darkness what we have learned in the light.

Having an eternal perspective will be radical and unheard of in this land of the short-term. It will be this that will transform your ability to thrive in Babylon. I know you are questioning if you can really do this, if you can be a disciple in these days. But if our faith is irrelevant when times get tough, then it amounts to nothing more than a fairy tale you tell children. If, however, it is the truth – if discipleship is necessary to thrive in real life, if God is real and if He is calling you to be His – then this changes everything. This makes your exile a make-or-break moment. Do you have a strong enough faith? Did you learn enough during the light to endure the dark? We'll come to these.

In one sense – through God's eyes – nothing has changed; we are always held by Him. But through our eyes, everything has changed; all the things normative to our faith have vanished. So now, today, we wonder if we are strong enough to endure.

Are we ... ? I don't think so.

It's time to grieve the loss of our city and of our nation, and to cry to the God of our ancestors. We must tell Him this mountain is too high for us; His ways are too high.

Daniel, I do not know how you are as you read this letter. Or how, when you hear about your father wailing, you will react. I do not know if they are treating you as prisoner or guest. But in my 22 years of living as a disciple, I have learned one key truth about weakness: when you're going to fall, fall in God's direction.

Asking, 'Am I strong enough?' is a bogus question for the disciple. It is only fools who think *their* faith is strong. Faith as its own entity is as unpredictable as pure luck. For it is not how much faith we have or how strong our faith is but *who* our faith is in that makes the difference. The great heroes of our history were not people of a blind faith but people who had great reason to believe.

For us, Daniel, what matters is not how we hold onto God but that we let the great God of heaven hold onto us. And so with our real history and with the real promises

God has given about our future, we too have great reason to believe. We have no empty hope.

*

Yet the conditions of your life will – at the very least – not be favourable and certainly far from your choosing. Nevertheless, God is with you and you can live an adventurous, purposeful life within the story God is telling. Allow Him to hold you up, to empower you to be pure in a corrupt generation.

It's tempting, when you're in the valley of the shadow, to fall away from God in the world's direction. That is, to fall into sin, thinking that though there would be a pain in rejecting your upbringing, at least you wouldn't then be so different from those around you. This would miss the target of real living. It would be a short-term gain for a long-term price. Idiotic and damning. You see, sin tells us a lie: that to really be free you should be free to sin. But this is like saying that to prove someone is healed you should make them sick again. It misses the whole point. You are healed so you can live a healthy life, not so you can be reinfected. God forgives our sins, not so we can sin all the more but so we can embrace the freedom His forgiveness offers.

Taking a step back to analyse things from a considered position will soon reveal it is sin that traps and God who frees. For God creates and then creates some more. And in this creation, there is space for total freedom. His kingdom is the only place you can live the adventure for which you were destined. To go against God is to sail against the wind – to restrict salvation's effect. But when you align yourself to the breath of His Spirit, you will begin to dream bigger dreams and live a fuller life.

So when you feel like you're going to fall, fall in God's direction. He is ready to uphold you, and full of grace.

Indeed, in this godly adventure there is a life not only of freedom but also of joy. Even now – even there where you are, even here where I am – my fear-filled hands can still answer what God wants for you. His desire is for you to live a significant life, with wide smiles and absolute assurance displaying God's brilliance throughout your days, free from the traps of sin and the weeds of the world. This is what I have learned in the light: God wants you to overflow with joy.

For our God is a party planner! Our festivals are not like those of the pagan nations around us, who hope vainly to grab their fake god's attention. Our God asks us to celebrate our actual salvation that happened in real history. Our faith is not a bunch of ideas tied together in a logical format. It is certainly not a children's fairy tale. No! As I watch this sunrise, I am convinced we have great reason to believe. Our faith is a response to what God has done, is doing and has promised to do for us. Celebrating and remembering in the same act has become the fashion of our formation, because God knows true freedom is celebrating the past when the present isn't as good. True hope is celebrating the future before it happens.

*

So the question is not, 'Is my faith strong enough?' but, 'What is my response to this God who has been and will continue to be my Redeemer?'

Will I live my life as part of His story?

Will I tell of His greatness?

Will I live distinctly for Him?

For it is He who calls you by name, He who has created you for a purpose, and He who invites you now into what will be a strange and wonderful partnership of seeing His kingdom come in Babylon.

Remember to pray for us, as we do for you.

Keep your eyes open,

Abel

PS I've included my prayer for this morning.

A morning prayer

Today is your day, God,
Not the people's,
Not Babylon's, not mine.
It is created by you and it is yours.

So, God, I also am yours.
May my work today be your work today.
Lord, I'm not stuck in a rut, I'm committed to a purpose
To live for you.

Teach me to climb.
I need stamina.
When my days feel like the mid-mountain strain and not the mountain top,
Give me the strength to embrace this adventure.

Drench my imagination with creativity.
May I live with tenacity.
Lord, save me from a chicken's life
For I long to live faithfully, courageously in the adventure of faith.

Steady my heart as I rise.
It is not if you are for us that I question
But if I am in line with you.
Invite me in again, dear God.

Who else is there but you?
You alone can rescue: lift my eyes.
You alone hold the nations: give me perspective.
You alone are God: I bow the knee.

As the sun rises, I rise
And I give you this day.
It is yours, all yours,
As am I.

To think about:

1. When have you not felt strong enough?
2. On a scale from 'I'm hiding my faith' to 'I'm unembarrassed about it' to 'I'm shouting it from the rooftops', how public are you about your faith? Think about these different settings: your family, your friends and your social media.
3. What did you really need to hear from this letter?

3

Where Is My Home?

'Am I only a God nearby,'
declares the L*ORD*,
'and not a God far away?'

(Jeremiah 23:23)

Dear Daniel,

I was 43 when you were born and only then beginning to call your father's house 'home'. You were born into one. For me home was always a concept, never a reality. When I was a boy, my parents were forced into servitude by debt, and just two years after a Jubilee year, when all debts are automatically forgiven. As you know, they died before their time, just as I was becoming a man. And so I began to work for your grandfather. I have had a privileged life but not a free one. While I've had elements of freedom here and there, and I'm by no means complaining of your family's treatment of me, humanly speaking I've never experienced the feeling of being in *my* home. It is God who has given me that opportunity – to be found; to be content in being His.

As you come to terms with the reality of being a captive, I want to pry open a dialogue most likely happening in your heart already – the conversation of where you belong. Living with one soil beneath your feet and your heart planted in another is the reality of your condition, but how can we ensure you make a home where you are?

The generations before us asked how they could call Jerusalem their real home with *this king or that judge or these people.* They would say, 'How can this be our promised land when there is "that idol" or "these practices" or "those voices" in our society?' Yet for those of us seeking to live as true disciples, being holy where you find yourself is the heart of godliness, even if you find yourself in Babylon.

The very essence of the human condition is about longing for 'home'. Every life tells this tale; every story contains an aching to be loved; every dream holds a vision of this peace.

And the truth our lives hinge on is that we belong to God. It is only when He is our God and we are His people that we will be fully alive, fully ourselves, fully free, fully at home. So while you might be asking, 'Where is my home?' a better question for you to ask is: 'How do I live my life with God, wherever I am?'

*

Your praying heart will throb for Jerusalem, but you must also begin praying for the place that dirties your knees as you kneel. You must begin calling Babylon home; to see how God is at work and participate in His plans; to live out your faith from this new place; to sing the songs of Zion in a Babylonian key; to worship the one true God as you work within your new Babylonian routines and roles. What a task living for God in exile will be. And that great visionary mind of yours, though born and raised in Israel, can also smell the eastern flowers, serve with a pagan king and love your Babylonian neighbour. As the noise of the city rises, you can still rest in who you are before God. We do not have to be exiles in our own hearts; we can be at home with God anywhere.

For me, I only really began to feel at home when your father trusted me with your upbringing. From that point, with significant purpose, my master's house began to feel homely. While, on first examination, you could say I've been homeless my entire life, I have felt at home here. Indeed, I don't want to leave now; your family *is* where I belong.

I wonder, in some way, if my experience of being a bond-servant – of which you have witnessed up close – could act as a humble example of exile for you. With it, perhaps you can begin to understand your own story, as you seek to live free under bondage.

You will get well treated – that's my guess anyway – but this will not make you any less a captive. However, in my prayers, I have seen you not only surviving in exile but thriving in a place where you belong – a place where you become who God intends you to be.

*

The truth is, 'Babylon' has always been part of our nation's story. We have always been in a sort of exile. Let me show you what I mean, because I fear in your absence from Jerusalem you will romanticise what it was like here. For when it comes to our return from exile, God has made it clear: 'If you, Israel, will return, then return to me' (Jeremiah 4:1).

Right from the start, Adam and Eve brought an end to our full partnership with God by doubting and disobeying His good commands. The new beginning with Noah and his family also failed in getting us back to God – again ending in naked shame. This built to a complete refusal of God in the Babel account: 'Let us build ourselves a city, with a tower that reaches to the heavens, so that we may make a name for ourselves' (Genesis 11:4). No partnership, just independence. Sheer selfish desire celebrated to the world.

While these are our stories, I want you to see Babylon in them. I'm sure it wouldn't take too much of a creative mind to imagine Nebuchadnezzar leading a rebuilding of the tower of Babel. Perhaps in your time he might try it! Because this is the pattern.

The tower of Babel resulted in all people being exiled throughout the world. And it seemed hopeless, until God whispered in Abram's ear. Abram accepted an invite from God, making our nation partial partners with Him again. We were called to be a unique people, who will bless the world.

In present-day Babylon we see a full refusal of this partnership as well. They may be building an empire and not a tower but it is the same story retold. God doesn't even get an acknowledgement! But remember how, in the story of the tower of Babel, God had to stoop to see what they were doing, so flimsy was their achievement. Likewise, no matter how those blue gates of Babylon dazzle you or how big the palaces are, God will have to crouch to see them. Babylon's grandeur is not the main thing that is happening in the world. Nebuchadnezzar is but a squatter of authority ignorantly calling his dominion an achievement. He misses the reality of God's reign.

And now you, Daniel, must make your home here among these pagan people in this city of terrible brilliance.

Keep your eyes open,

Abel

PS I attach a section of the letter from our prophet Jeremiah to you and your comrades. (Perhaps you have already received the full letter?) My letters you can view as suggestions but Jeremiah's letter is God's voice. Live it out. Settle in Babylon and find your home in God. He has plans to prosper you – seek Him with all your heart.

> *This is what the* Lord *Almighty, the God of Israel, says to all those I carried into exile from Jerusalem to Babylon: 'Build houses and settle down; plant gardens and eat what they produce. Marry and have sons and daughters; find wives for your sons and give your daughters in marriage, so that they too may have sons and daughters. Increase in number there; do not decrease. Also, seek the peace and prosperity of the city to which I have carried you into exile. Pray to the* Lord *for it, because if it prospers, you too will prosper' …*
>
> *'For I know the plans I have for you,' declares the* Lord*, 'plans to prosper you and not to harm you, plans to give you hope and a future. Then you will call on me and come and pray to me, and I will listen to you. You will seek me and find me when you seek me with all your heart. I will be found by you,' declares the* Lord*.*
>
> *(Jeremiah 29:4–7, 11–14)*

To think about:

1. Where do you consider your home town to be?
2. Abel writes, 'The very essence of the human condition is about longing for "home". Every life tells this tale; every story contains an aching to be loved; every dream holds a vision of this peace.' Do you agree with his statement about the nature of who we are? How does this point us to God?
3. Read over Jeremiah's letter to the exiles. What stands out, and how does it encourage you today?

4

How Does My Worldview Differ?

... they do not even know how to blush.

(Jeremiah 6:15)

Dear Daniel,

The fires are still burning. You'd think the Babylonians would leave the weak cattle for the remnant but they spill their blood and then just burn them. *Who are these people you will be living with?*

I imagine we have seen them at their worst. Still gloating over their victory at Carchemish, they are at their most powerful and least compassionate. We are a trophy nation to add to the pile on their victory lap. But what is the difference between them and us, between their worldview and ours?

A worldview is the way we view the world. Ours has been shaped by the Scriptures, by God acting in our history and promising us a future. Babylon will have their own worldview, formed by the stories they tell about themselves. So what becomes of a nation built on the unrepentant ideologies of power, wealth and desire? When you dig under the gleam of their achievements and expose the subconscious foundation, you will find very little basis for their ideology, except the desire to revolt against God's authority.

There are three fundamentals to the authority of God: creation, the future and our ultimate purpose. Each of these are God's possession. He alone can create, direct the future and give purpose. The Babylonians, who refuse to partner with God, are independent – secular. And, unwilling to partner with God, they instead try to achieve authority by opposing His ways. They will not articulate it in this way, of course, but this is my attempt to understand why they live with such sophisticated barbarism. Let me explain more:

- Since they cannot create life and refuse to know the One who does, they kill. They kill their enemies instead of learning to live in peace. I have even heard of them killing babies who don't fit their criteria of health and appearance. They may even claim the killing as *modern*, or progressive, when it all is just a pretence for control.
- Since they do not know the future and refuse to know the One who does, they strategise, plan and 'go forth and conquer', all to fancy power.
- Since they cannot find purpose and refuse to know the One who gives it, they join what's popular. With no foundation they work towards bogus goals, like a child

trying to build a better pebble tower than their friend, not realising that both their towers will one day fall.

We, however, are invited to partner in God's creation, to work towards a better future and to live out our purpose, simply by saying yes to God.

*

Yet we do not deal with society as a whole. We deal with individuals who follow along, just 'trying to fit in', just 'doing my job'. Here is the snare for the sluggard – thinking the majority is right, with no conviction for what *right* is.

Daniel, be alert! This land has a foliage thick, dark but impressive. It has grown over time in the quagmire of the rat race, often given the name 'careerism'. For the individual – of whom you'll deal with mostly – a career is a worthy pursuit. Yet it often ignores what their job actually does, what kind of a society it builds. This is different from our understanding of having a purpose under God. Careerism depersonalises people; it seeks to functionalise human souls to have roles instead of responsibilities, promotions instead of protections, 'winner gets all' instead of 'all in this together'. It halts us from doing something truly significant by just encouraging us to be better than the next best person. Careerism can promise success but rob you of what's important.

It feeds a human machine called the 'economy'. While not harmful in itself, this is a prize insecure rulers use to coax people's hearts towards a nationalistic outlook – and the rejection of God on a tribal scale. We've witnessed the gnarling teeth of nationalistic pride during this invasion. During times of peace, nationalism will remain sly under the disguise of the common consensus.

Nationalism ultimately exists for human glory. 'Look what we have done,' they will say of their accomplishments. They will raise their flags when their achievements tell a satisfying story. But when things go south, none will stand to say, 'I did it.' When things do go wrong, and the darkness is exposed, the outraged public will blame an entity individuals can only call '*they*'. *They* are taking our freedom; *they* are bringing in a liberal regime; the *system* is biased. The common man will exclaim, 'I was only doing my job.'

It takes the humility of repentance to acknowledge that what is wrong with the world is *me.*

The secular person is oblivious, morally sleepwalking their way through the system. When you pull back the veneer of professionalism and peer under the surface of secular society, you will see a middle finger directed towards the heavens, and no-one to blame for putting it there.

This is far removed from the life of virtue, responsibility and honour that comes from living under God. You, Daniel, rooted in love with the Scriptures pulsing through your veins, will be on display. The sheer uniqueness of your priorities will be noticed as you work not from the desire for wealth but as a person of principle. This may result in threat, demotion or misunderstanding. It may also result in success, promotion and responsibility. Either way, it is the only way to live a significant life – a free life.

It *is* possible to be a captive yet free. I have lived that story. It is also possible to be in Babylon yet represent the kingdom of God. *You* must live this one.

If I were you, the main difference I would feel is the people with whom you are living. In Jerusalem you were with a mixture of people, some devout, some distracted but all zigzagging in God's direction. And, of course, you had your family. My heart breaks for you; my prayers are with you. No amount of letters, ideas or clever perspectives will help you here. It is just so sad they are not with you. And I am so sorry.

Keep your eyes open,

Abel

To think about:

1. Where do you see a clash between the world around you and a biblical worldview?
2. Abel is trying to prepare Daniel for a society drastically different from the one he grew up in. It was an instant change. Our society is changing all the time. How would you compare your community to Abel's critique of Babylon?
3. What would help you become 'rooted in love with the Scriptures pulsing through your veins'?

5

What Else Should I Be Asking?

How can we sing the songs of the L*ORD*
while in a foreign land?

(Psalm 137:4)

Dear Daniel,

Before we move onto our next group of letters, I want to say one more thing: while there are many differences between Jerusalem and Babylon, we have lived with some form of these differences all our lives.

If no invasion was happening and we were all here in Judah, we'd be longing for a king like Josiah again. Go back a couple of generations and you'd hear the same thing. It's been the story of our people to be unsatisfied with where we are when that is our situation. 'The Promised Land' is like a shimmering oasis we never quite reach. Until *that* great dawn appears, when our tears will be wiped away, there will always be a sense we are not quite home. Not yet.

That is why, when Israel felt more like God's kingdom, we felt more at home. When our nation went wrong – and God knows we've gone wrong – even the most dire of our priests would say, 'This is not *the* Promised Land.' It is not a matter of geography but reign; it is not who occupies our land but who we give our allegiance to that matters. We are, by God's design, always free to choose who governs our hearts and we should not allow the sword to sway our faithfulness. And anyway, who's to say God's kingdom is not active in Babylon? Indeed, maybe more active?

Ah, I wish I could sit with you and see your reaction to this – you were always good with questions. I think that's why you have grown into the young man you've become – the questions someone asks are often more telling than the answers they give.

So here are a few to ask yourself:

Where is God?

Is God more present in Jerusalem or in Babylon?

Does God reign in Babylon?

Is God with you today?

What is the difference between living for God in Jerusalem and in Babylon?

Will you live as a citizen of God's kingdom in the country of Babylon?

The darker the culture, the brighter you'll shine. And while 'they do not even know how to blush' (Jeremiah 6:15), an unembarrassed godly life is a powerful weapon against their sophisticated evil and pointed swords. I believe your witness could turn even Nebuchadnezzar's heart to God.

*

Over next few weeks, as you acclimatise to your move, I wonder if these are the best first steps?

1. Stay humble: humble enough to ask questions; to seek wisdom; to discern the path of a disciple in a pagan nation; to know Babylon is big and you are a tiny part of it.
2. Stay hungry: hungry enough to seek God from a foreign land; to establish a rhythm of devotion; to know Babylon is ready to hear the good news from a persuaded disciple.
3. Seek fellowship: fellowship you can be at home with; faithful friends who will inspire you to live a significant life, knowing this adventure will take all the help you can get.

Keep your eyes open,

Abel

To think about:

1. What questions do you have about living out your faith?
2. Which of the three 'next steps' would you like to make a priority in your own life?
3. What can you do today that would help you take a step in that direction?

TIME TO DISCUSS

> *Then he called the crowd to him along with his disciples and said: 'Whoever wants to be my disciple must deny themselves and take up their cross and follow me.'*
>
> *(Mark 8:34)*

You've got some decisions to make. I hope Abel's letters are helping give perspective. Ultimately, though, they are only to show how the freedom and faithfulness we see in Daniel's life can inspire us to live for the kingdom of God in our time and in our place. Daniel has lived his life; now we must live ours.

Imagine the captain of a ship that is sailing through pleasant water. When suddenly the ship enters dangerous rocky waters, the captain's focus must sharpen so they can navigate the way ahead. We too are at a turning point in history for followers of Jesus: moving into exile. There is the need for clear thinking, open eyes and a boldness in our faith. Autopilot will not get you through. Abel has given Daniel some primary thoughts in these letters, using questions to spark his imagination towards robust thinking – thinking free from fear but aware of danger.

We must listen to Abel's call to Daniel, to 'keep your eyes open', so we don't get distracted or scared of the rocky waters ahead but keep our gaze on Jesus. Because He is here, He continues to work, continues to save. And He says to you, 'Take courage! It is I. Don't be afraid.' (Matthew 14:27)

Guide for meeting together

1. Go back over the previous letters and discuss what parts struck you.
2. Take it in turns to pick one of the questions 'to think about' at the end of each letter and share your thoughts.
3. Discuss these questions:
    - What do you think is changing in our culture?
    - What are the key questions Christians should be asking during this moment in history?
    - Considering the next steps Abel gives to Daniel in the previous letter, what next steps can you take to embrace in all its fullness the life Jesus is offering to you?
4. Pray together to close.

SECTION TWO

—

The Crossroads

This is what the LORD *says:*

'Stand at the crossroads and look;
ask for the ancient paths,
ask where the good way is, and walk in it,
and you will find rest for your souls.'

(Jeremiah 6:16)

6

Standing at the Crossroads

Like a scarecrow in a cucumber field,
their idols cannot speak ...
But the Lord is the true God;
he is the living God, the eternal King.
(Jeremiah 10:5, 10)

Stand at the crossroads ...
(Jeremiah 6:16)

Dear Daniel,

It was one of those nights where the earth held the heat of the day, the air still. We listened to the words of our prophet, Jeremiah, as the sun set. It was there I knew for the first time that behind the mess of our social history and religious institutions lived real truth. The Lord spoke to me as clear as I'm writing this. It was my conversion moment.

The pleasant evening did not mirror our prophet's tongue, whose sermon rose in the warm air, travelled across the crowd and hit me like a hammer to the chest. I exchanged one life for another that day. I went from the mundane existence of a passive, obedient lifestyle to really believing – to really being His.

I wish you could have been there. Jeremiah had a way of exclaiming the truth that gave the Word of God its weight, its ferocity – the sharp edge of divine revelation exposed your heart. He made me feel like I was standing at an actual crossroads – I could see it in my mind's eye. He asked us to look from a different perspective; to take a step back from our daily living and assess where we were at.

Jeremiah asked questions like: have you let the truth take root in your heart? Can you identify the ancient paths of faith that have held disciples for generations? Do you know where the good way is? And will you walk in it? He was passionate because he believed we could be saved – not from the invasion, but from believing their lies.

I became a disciple that day – 22 years ago. I gave my yes to God.

It was your Father who brought me along that day. On the walk home we talked it out. Not only did I become a believer that evening, but your Dad and I became friends. I was still his servant, of course, but we were friends nevertheless. It confirmed to me that it was the right decision to ask to remain with your family after the debt was settled.

Today, I too invite you to consider the crossroads you

are at. You are walking the way of faith but now, cutting straight across it, will be Babylon's way. You have a choice. And I hope to help you understand that choice. Which way will eat you and which will give you rest for your soul? The way of Babylon has questionable beginnings and doesn't know where it is going. The road of our faith begins in creation and ends in eternal security. Comparison, as always, is the mother of clarity.

*

Let's imagine the crossroads you are at as two bodies of water: the movement of God and the movement of Babylon, colliding in one rapid of confusion and decisions.

This is the rapid you are in.

Do you remember when your father took you to Joppa? I think you were nine or ten. It was well worth the four-hour trek – even for me! He, of course, had been at the port many times to trade. But the seasons were turning from late spring to summer and there was space for leisure, so he decided to bring us along. It's unlikely you'll see it again. And you will be a lot more than a day away from the ocean in Babylon.

Time passed like a darting rabbit as we enjoyed the waves. On the way home you began to tell your father 'what the waves do' ... as if he'd never seen them before!

Do you remember what you said? You described the sea like hands that caught you and pushed you into shore: 'It's like they *want* you to swim towards the beach. And if you try to swim sideways or out to sea, they just keep throwing you back. But if you launch yourself with a wave, you're carried in the current; you're light, flying freeeee.' I remember it word for word! Your dad winked at me as if to say, 'I told you it'd be worth it!'

I recall this memory to help us consider the difference between God's way and Babylon's way. I do not see these crossroads – these waters meeting – as equal. In comparison to what God is doing throughout the centuries with His people and in the world – an authoritative, long-term movement like an ocean – Babylon is exposed as just a trickle of power. This crossroads is not two equal rivers meeting, with one as strong as the other. No! It is more like a river coming side on to an incoming tide.

It's easy to move with the current, but difficult (or, for a nine-year-old, impossible) to swim against. You might make some progress, but ultimately, no matter how great a swimmer you might be, the tide is going a certain direction. If you don't move with it, you'll lose the fight.

For you personally, it may feel like you're faced with a *tide of opinions* or that you'll have to *swim against the tide* in Babylon. This may be true at present but I am talking about a bigger current than current affairs, an older tide than Babylonian culture. They are modern only in their own eyes, thinking their philosophy is the new wave for a new era. Little do they know that, with the backdrop of history, their power is but an exaggerated ripple in the grand tide of God-guided history.

Our Scriptures, you see, are not only to give us a temporal perspective. They also give us the reality – the truth – of the world. Of our history. Of God. Of us. They ensure we don't get tossed about by the side currents of our age but that we learn to align ourselves with the direction of God's will.

Like trying to swim against the tide, each secular endeavour, each individual rebellion is eventually engulfed into the movement of the story of God. So we, as His people, must learn not to align ourselves with the current wave of popular opinion or to bow to the current pressure of our circumstances. Instead, we must align ourselves with the giant movement of God across the ages. The direction of that tide may be harder to discern at times than a quick splash in the face from the current contemporary culture, but it is the surer, truer reality. It is as we align ourselves to God's will that we can learn to live 'light and freeeee', enjoying life like you enjoyed those waves at Joppa.

I trust that considering your crossroads enables you to live from a place of radical conviction. There is no need to hate or envy other cultures; we are simply called to minister to them in prayerful compassion. Daniel, we can be audacious in our faithfulness when we understand there is a God in heaven who makes Nebuchadnezzar's authority look like a drop in the ocean compared to the swells and pull of His moving tide.

Keep your eyes open,

Abel

To think about:

1. What crossroad moments have you had in your life so far? What Bible passages were important during those times?
2. Abel is trying to give Daniel some perspective to begin translating his faith into his new life in Babylon. Lots of practical stuff will come later but, at this point, what kind of emotions do you think Daniel would have felt when reading this letter?

7

Balancing the Tension

So do not listen to your prophets who tell you …
'You will not serve the king of Babylon.'
(Jeremiah 27:9)

… and look …
(Jeremiah 6:16)

Dear Daniel,

While the movement of God is the ultimate movement, this rapid you are in will cause significant splashes. I am not suggesting Babylon will be easy to withstand. A splash in the face can disorientate even the most balanced of men if it comes at the right angle and speed. We would be flippant to think there is no risk of you losing your footing. So do not misread yesterday's perspective as a dumbing down of the real threat Babylon represents. It is the reason for these letters, after all.

*

There will be considerable skill involved to balance the tension you will face. I see this as a tension between your two primary callings held within a new context.

Your new context

I heard from Baruch that when Nebuchadnezzar entered our temple, he asked, 'Where is Israel's god? ... Is this not your temple?'

Of course, while it perplexes us, Nebuchadnezzar's notion of gods is purely of deities that humans create. Statues. When he didn't see an idol in the centre of our temple, he thought it was a godless temple.

He was hoping to bring our God with him to Babylon, to display his *acceptance* of our religion. The concept (and I doubt anyone dared to try and explain it to him) of us worshipping *the* only uncreated God, who has revealed Himself to us, would be as foreign to him as Babylon is for you. The fact your faith is not an opinion but a celebration of a real relationship would be unheard of – to Nebuchadnezzar and the Babylonians.

I believe you will be confronted with the notion that your faith isn't real or reasonable or true, but is simply part of your upbringing. In a cosmopolitan centre like Babylon, worship is given a thorough demotion. Your religion will be referred to as your 'culture'. Your new neighbours will see your faith in God as just one of many things that makes Daniel Daniel! Truth will be relative for them, identity invented and worship just personal opinion.

This is the backdrop I see – the context in which you will live out your devotion to the Lord.

Two primary callings

Within this context you are invited to live out your two primary callings: 1. God is asking you to seek the peace and prosperity of this city. 2. He is also asking you to be faithful to Him. Holding these two callings in tension will be no stride around Galilee. You must serve to prosper a society while maintaining radical doubt about its foundations and direction. You must be true to God, displaying and developing His love across a city distanced from the peace He brings.

The pull to go too far in one direction will be strong – to break one calling in favour of the other. This balance will require steady contemplation. But, for the most part, you will know the right answer – it will be a matter of having the bravery to stand, the skill to settle or the humility to serve when the time comes.

*

Some of our rituals are indeed mere cultural expressions, superfluous to an active faith, but living as God's people is the central reality that governs our days as disciples. And so there are key aspects of our faith you must carry unchanged into Babylon – they are essential to your discipleship. There is truth we must never forget; truth to impress on our foreheads. I want to keep Jeremiah's words as a guide into these truths. We have 'stood at the crossroads ... and looked'. Now we must 'ask for the ancient paths, ask where the good way is'. Then, finally, we can consider the choice we have to 'walk in it'.

In tomorrow's letter we will consider these unchanging truths. They are the foundations to the ancient paths we walk on as disciples. These paths lead to the good way.

Keep your eyes open,

Abel

To think about:

1. How does the context Daniel was in match the context in which you follow Jesus?
2. Can you think of a time in this coming year where you will need the bravery to stand, the skill to settle and the humility to serve? Do you feel a similar tension to Daniel? How does the tension between the 'two primary callings' surface in your life?

8

God Creates Us

How gladly would I treat you like my children …
(Jeremiah 3:19)

… ask for the ancient paths,
ask where the good way is …
(Jeremiah 6:16)

Dear Daniel,

When you look to the Negev Desert, you will see it is crisscrossed with paths made by generations of wild horses. These horses are unbound, yet together they form paths. They have total freedom to go anywhere across the wide expanse, yet they know that to get to pasture without breaking a foot or stumbling to their peril, the path trod by their forefathers is the best way to embrace the freedom they're afforded. As disciples we must be able to identify the paths that carry believers, to know the direction of the tide, so we too can really live free as God intended.

When we submit ourselves to God and to His ways, we will find ourselves in a spacious place – salvation. We become part of the family of God and so find home, hope and wholeness. Life was not supposed to be broken or sinful. We were not set free from the Garden of Eden; that garden was freedom. *We* brought the sin and brokenness into the world; *God* is working to free us from its prisons, empowering us to live holy lives today.

An eagle is carried by her strong wings high into the air and skilfully hovers to scan the landscape. May we soar up on our knowledge of the Torah, hover from a distance and consider the main path that has carried disciples towards godly living over the centuries.

There are three grounding truths here that act as the foundation to these ancient paths: we live in response to a *God who creates*, a *God who rescues* and a *God who guides*. A holy life is achieved by accepting the reality of these truths. We live out the adventure birthed by our faith as we respond to our creating, rescuing and guiding God. Let's take them one at a time. As you read, impress these truths in your memory – never forget these things. Let's begin with living in response to a God who has created us.

God creates us; we live as a created people

In the beginning, God created the world and it was good. Indeed, after forming us in His image, he declared it very good. God creates each of us at a particular time and set us in a specific place where He invites us into partnership with Him. This was as true for Adam as it is for you. Your time is not then, but now. Your place is not Eden, but Babylon. Nevertheless, you are an image-bearer of God and invited into partnership.

We know that our fundamental *identity*, *purpose* and *relationship* comes from our Creator – they are gifts not inventions. We are created as someone, for a reason, by our heavenly Father. This is at total odds with secular society, which does not have this bedrock of understanding. In Babylon, not knowing the truth about their creation, they attempt to conceive their own identity, purpose and relationships rather than receive these as a gift from their Creator. The result is a damning trade, exchanging a God-centred life for a self-centred existence, as we will next see.

Created identity is traded for self-invention

It may come under the guise of self-discovery or idol-making or 'becoming who you are', but make no mistake – none of these cultural terms talk about receiving or accepting who you are. The end result is confusion not simplicity, self-doubt not self-assurance, pride not humility, greed not generosity – you become holey not holy. As the unbelieving world asks, 'Who am I?' we can rest in the answer: 'I know who I am. I'm an image-bearer of God himself.' We are God's people – this is our fundamental identity.

Created purpose is traded for self-promotion

Without a God-given purpose, the only thing left for society to assume is that *you* are the reason for your existence. In the end, this causes a sense of worthlessness not meaning, hollowness not wholeness, caution not courage, nervousness not nobility. As the unbelieving world asks, 'What am I supposed to do with my life?' we can simply acknowledge our responsibility to be partners with God in caring for His world, raising families and ministering to those around us as we live under God's blessing. We are God's witnesses – this is our fundamental purpose.

Created relationship is traded for self-assertion

Everyone longs to be known and loved, but when each person you meet is incapable of knowing or loving you fully, you try to just accept yourself. To your horror, you then find that same incapability in your own heart. Instead of being carried through life in a relationship with a God of power who loves you, life will begin to feel like a famished road, eating away your youth. We react by asserting ourselves; we selfishly claim our rights. The end result is rejection not acceptance, treating people as assets not friends, feeling like a stranger not known, being lost not found. As the unbelieving world asks, 'Am I loved?' we can wake in the morning, kneel beside our bed and engage with our provider God, who loves and speaks to us as our Father. We are in God's family – this is our fundamental relationship.

*

Get these fundamentals right and the inner self quiets. You will feel breath in your lungs once again and find rest for your soul.

The first foundation of the ancient paths we walk on as disciples is that we live not as a questioning people but as a created people. We know the One who has created us longs to treat us not as slaves but as His children.

To remember this, we take Sabbath: a day where we acknowledge we didn't create the world, nor do we sustain it; a day when the journey isn't a journey but a place. So we stop, do no work and remind ourselves to live a God-centred life rather than the self-centred existence of the unbelieving world.

Daniel, I'm going to sign off here. I was hoping to write one long letter regarding all three foundations, but I have to move during the night. I am currently in the hut outside the olive grove. I will seal this letter and put it in the bag. I go to fetch more parchment in the morning.

Keep your eyes open,

Abel

To think about:

1. How does an understanding of the foundational principles of Christian living help us embrace the freedom Jesus brings?
2. Go back over this letter and circle one key sentence you would like to remember.
3. Abel draws a comparison between Daniel and 'the unbelieving world'. Where, in the book of Daniel, do you see him remembering his identity (as one of God's people), living out his purpose (as a witness for God) and committing to his relationship (as part of God's family)?

9

God Rescues Us

I am with you and will save you.

(Jeremiah 30:11)

… ask for the ancient paths,
ask where the good way is …

(Jeremiah 6:16)

Dear Daniel,

I am in the olive press now. I hope to move back to my cabin if the city quiets. I went to your father's store to get the parchments last night. We managed to speak for a short while, arranging to meet each morning before dawn for prayer. He is still grieving your capture. He is planning to take what he has left and leave this looted city of grieving mothers. He wants me to go with him. Unsure if he could make it to Babylon, he is considering Egypt. We fear that when the armies come back in a year or two, as they have indicated, your younger siblings will be taken also – or go missing like your mother the day before you were chosen.

I would rather not write you these things and have considered leaving them out, but your father and I agree that it's important you know. For our faith isn't lived in a vacuum but in the reality of the conditions where we find ourselves. We need to be honest before God, to come bounded or bruised to worship Him who liberates and heals. Being true is our part; rescue is His.

It is, of course, easier to talk about how God rescues us in the past tense – sometime in the future, on the far side of occupation. But it's truer to say it now, before we know the end.

The second foundation of these ancient paths we walk on as disciples is we live as rescued people. Like a husband who would defend his wife at any cost, the God to whom we belong redeems us at any cost.

God rescues us; we live as a rescued people

We don't get far in the Torah before sin enters the world. 'The Fall', as some call it, happens. With Adam and Eve's rebellion, our identity gets distorted, our purpose skewed and our relationship broken.

This matches our life experience. No sooner do we see creation than we notice it's gone wrong. We look out and breathe in the beauty, but in the same breath we have to acknowledge this place isn't whole – not even when we look at Jerusalem, our family or our own heart. A sickness, fatal to our souls, envelops us and taints the world around us. We can try to follow God's rules, but before long we come to realise we can't. This place is broken; I am broken; we need rescue.

Four words: Sin. Pain. Brokenness. Death.

Each of these is so prevalent in our society – no-one would deny their existence. Yet do any of them feel normal? Do we wake in the morning and long to be sinned against, to feel pain or brokenness? Indeed, is it ever a *normal* day when death comes?

What I'm trying to expose here is how our sin has caused every condition that feels at odds to life. Our fallen nature is unnatural; its alien qualities make us less alive. I've said it before but it is sin that traps and God who frees. This is why King David says, 'my bones wasted away through my groaning all day long' (Psalm 32:3).

We, like David, waste away feeling sin's piercing sadness in our bones. We need to give it – yes, *give it*! – to God. Give Him our broken, skewed and distorted lives. He is not longing to punish; He is longing to forgive, to recreate in us a pure heart. We cannot wriggle from sin or hide from its consequences. We cannot keep digging to get out of the pit – we need to be lifted out. The curse must be uncursed, the story rewritten. Our dead souls need not bandages but resurrection.

This forgiveness God offers is not advice or help; it is total restoration – full grace. And we can depend on this because of who God is. Our God rescues us. We are the people He rescues. We can trust He knows what He is doing.

*

In the exodus from Egypt, God didn't dismiss our sin or ignore the sin-soaked world in which we were enslaved. The sin was taken on with seriousness but His mercy is quicker than His anger.

He rescues us in both *grace* and *truth*. It is grace because we don't deserve it. It is truth because God deals with the sin. The Passover lamb was killed so that the Israelites might be spared. The angel of death was allowed to descend so that Egypt and her god might be judged. Together grace and truth pointed to the mercy of God; the angel of death saw the Lamb and asked for no more. Our freedom was born from that great unlikely marriage of forgiveness and justice. And our God continues to redeem us: the stories of His mercy will overlap until the day of the Lord, when the Messiah will come to rescue us in one final tsunami of sacrifice, forgiveness and freedom.

God's forgiveness, then, changes our relationship with the wrong in the world. It is transformed from one of pointing a judgemental finger to one of confession and grace. We know *we* are what is wrong with this place and we know our God will forgive us, inviting us to bring Shalom to our community.

This is at total odds with secular society. Babylonian people will also feel the weight of sin and the fear of death. But not accepting the God who rescues, they will react to the sin, pain, brokenness and death in two main ways: they will call it good or hide it.

To call bad 'good' involves celebrating what is wrong. This leaves the heart twisted and society in knots. Calling wrong 'right' does not make it right, and the dying soul will suffer his foolishness in the end.

Hiding from our brokenness will be seen in an effort to appear young or a drive for perfection. It involves shaming what is different, leaving the heart hard and society a masked parade. Concealing pain doesn't deal with it, but the unrepentant soul would rather salt his wounds than surrender his pride.

The result is a damning trade, exchanging a God-rescued life for a sin-spiralling death.

As the unbelieving world seeks perfection, we seek forgiveness. They mould their truth around how they want to live; we mould how we are to live around the truth. They will glorify or lie about their sin; we can confess it at the altar and walk away free.

When you know that God has and will rescue you, all that is left is to live a life that says thank you. Honour, I believe, is the correct term. Thankfulness is the starting place of genuine discipleship; honouring God is the lifestyle it births.

The second foundation of the ancient path we walk on as disciples is that we live not as an anxious people, but as a rescued people.

To remember this, we celebrate Passover. It reminds us not only of our rescue from Egypt but of the redemption that needs to happen in our own hearts as God enacts salvation for us.

Keep your eyes open,

Abel

To think about:

1. When did you realise you needed Jesus to rescue you from sin and its consequences?
2. Abel's letters are set around 605 BC, before Jesus came to rescue us. Daniel, and the rest of the Old Testament, points forward to this coming Saviour. Circle each sentence in Abel's letter that reminds you of Jesus.
3. The Hebrew people celebrated Passover. Christians celebrate communion. Jesus invites us to see communion as the new Passover celebration, with Him as the once-for-all sacrifice (see Mark 14:12–26). How can we ensure communion is a genuine act of remembering what Jesus has done for us?

10

God Guides Us

I will give you shepherds after my own heart, who will lead you with knowledge and understanding.
(Jeremiah 3:15)

... ask for the ancient paths,
ask where the good way is ...
(Jeremiah 6:16)

Dear Daniel,

We are in the place of faith. And if we're honest, we do not know what the horizon holds. You do, however, have a choice: to continue to trust the God in whom you have great reason to believe, or to forget about Him, loosen your grip and step off the ancient paths. To make that step, I would argue, is a much bigger step of faith than to continue on it. It would be to surf the splash rather than the tide. Having stories of faith rewarded is a beautiful gift hindsight affords. But for now, it is time to trust.

God's Word often speaks the contradiction to reality. When there was only darkness, God spoke, 'Let there be light', and it was from that word light broke through. Before His declaration, there was no evidence of the light. What you currently see shows Israel as an unfavoured, forgotten nation. We might wonder, if God is leading us, why would He lead us here? Yet God still says, 'I will be your God and you will be my people' (Jeremiah 7:23).

We've been building these three foundations of discipleship – these ancient paths we walk on. God creates us – yes, He does! We can see that clearly and it gives us a wholly different perspective. God rescues us – yes, He does! And as you enter this foreign land, we can find peace by knowing our God will rescue us, not only from our current problem but from our fundamental problems of sin and death.

Finally, God guides us. This is the most difficult to recognise. God's perspective is so different from ours, yet He invites us to follow. He does not coerce; He calls. It is an invitation to partnership, not an indictment of puppetry He imposes on our lives. God guides us – yes, He does! And while at times we cannot make sense of all this, we are invited to trust Him. This is the third foundation of the ancient path we walk on as disciples. God creates us. God rescues us. God guides us.

God guides us; we live as a guided people

We are not saved and then stuck; we are not rescued for nothing. Our ancestors were not left on the safe side of the Red Sea to figure things out for themselves, and neither are you. God created you, Daniel. He rescued you. And now He will guide you.

The priests carrying the ark were knee-deep in the River Jordan before God revealed their next step to the Promised Land. Likewise, I wonder how often our lives are on the verge of a miracle, if only we had the faith to get our feet wet. If we truly want to live out the adventure of faith God is guiding us into, we must become members of the soggy sandal society. We must be counted with those priests, who were willing to step into the Jordan before it had opened up. At times, Daniel, you must be willing to risk it all if you are to live out your calling to be godly in this foreign land.

As we've seen, the Torah does indeed show us how we are created and rescued, but most space is given to our guidance. There are great volumes of God's instructions and Moses' sermons – sometimes repetitive, sometimes fresh. It is as if God knew we would need most help accepting this foundation.

We are created at a particular time and in a specific place. We are rescued in grace and truth. And the way God guides us is just as wholesomely basic: He guides us as part of a commissioned community. Faith is personal but it is not lived individually; we are in this together.

The question is: who else will be singing the songs of Zion by the rivers of Babylon? What does this commissioned community look like without the priests and the temple, the prophets and the politics of Jerusalem? This is a hard question as you navigate the path of godliness through your exile. It will look different to and a lot smaller than it did in Jerusalem. But if you commit to follow God with even a handful of believers – as a commissioned community – you will find the guidance of God clearer, your steps bolder and your faith will have soil to grow.

This is at total odds with secular society. For them, independence, not community, is prized. Life is about following your heart not transforming your heart. As the unbelieving world tries to climb a social ladder, trampling on their comrades to get ahead, we can go for a walk with fellow believers, encouraging each other to live honest lives worthy of our calling. We are to be witnesses to the nations, assured of our position before God as created and rescued members of His family.

*

God guides us and our response is to follow Him in the company of believers for the glory of God. The final foundation of the ancient path we walk on as disciples is that we are to live not as an independent person but as a guided people – as the commissioned community sent by God to bless the world.

To remember we are guided, we teach our children the stories of how we have been guided so far and give them the sign of the covenant, trusting that God will continue to guide them also. We give the prophets our listening ear and open the Scriptures with expectancy to hear not only old truths but fresh direction. This reminds us that we belong not to the world but to God, that we've been marked as His.

*

These three truths form the baseline for our discipleship as believers. They provide the foundation of the path you will have to navigate. Please don't forget them. Each time you feel yourself slipping from holiness, remind yourself whose you are, how He saved you and that He is with you wherever you go.

Babylon will be impressive. However, it will have pride but no roots; it will be large but hollow, loud but empty. There are those who will try and fight against Babylon but this would be contrary to our calling. We are to seek peace and to pray for its prosperity. So we will bring change not with swords and spears but rather with wisdom. We are wisdom warriors who know there is a God in heaven and who exhibit kingdom-centred living to tell the longer story.

Keep your eyes open,

Abel

To think about:

1. Abel writes, 'At times, Daniel, you must be willing to risk it all if you are to live out your calling to be godly in this foreign land.' What examples do you see of this in action in Daniel's life?
2. When have you known guidance from God?
3. What is the relationship between guidance and faith – in both Daniel's life and in your life?
4. God guides us as part of a commissioned community to play our part in making disciples and seeing His kingdom come. What are some ways you can play your part in both your local and the global church?

11

Your Choice

Take note of the highway,
the road that you take.

(*Jeremiah 31:21*)

... and walk in it,
and you will find rest for your souls.

(*Jeremiah 6:16*)

Dear Daniel,

Sometimes the obvious choice and the difficult choice are the same. We have stood at the crossroads and considered the foundations of the ancient paths we walk on as disciples. It is time for you to make a decision, to ask where the good way is and to choose to walk in it. On that warm evening when the words of Jeremiah first hit me, I decided to become a true disciple, but many – indeed most – did not.

To help you make this decision with clarity, I want to dismantle a pressure you will face, expose what I think your main temptation is and highlight God's invitation. Daniel, this is completely your choice and you *must* choose. If you do not, Babylon will choose for you.

The pressure to blend in

Why all the effort to live by the truth? Would it not be easier to just go with the majority?

We want bargains, we want an easy life and we are attracted to the idea of blending in with the world. In doing so, we forget the arch enemy of faith is not doubt but apathy. Whether fear or a lack of backbone is the driving force behind blending in, before we know it, we are living the same adventure-less, short-term existence as everyone else. And we become irrelevant in our society by the very nature of being the same. No distinctiveness. No voice. No ability to bless.

Blending in is living a life someone else thinks is a good idea. But there is only one way to be a complete human: to live freely with God in the space of salvation.

God is the reality that makes your life real, the strength that makes you strong, the story you live in, the hope you hold. Babylonian culture will attempt to mould you into something more like a societal pet than a free person; a puppet rather than someone who responds to God in authentic individuality. To walk these ancient paths of freedom you must squash your fear, cast aside your ego and instead inhabit a God-centred reality. You can enjoy the new games and clothes of Babylon, but within it all remember God, not the world, is your guide.

Would you rather ride on a horse or a rat? Why saddle up on the weak, temporary story of a society when the wondrous love of God is there to mount? How regretful to take your unique influence and waste it by fitting in. How sad to wake up one day realising you've lived the wrong story. God has created you for much more than monotonous living. Please, Daniel, do not bow to the pressure to blend in.

The temptation to bite back

As I watch what they are doing to our country, I feel the urge to hate. I am faced with it most days as I watch this soon-to-be smouldering city weep its wrecking. While this same temptation is present for you, after some time and some healing, your anger will become less noticeable. But in its place could grow an embittered glare with which you will view your new neighbours.

Forgiveness is a humbling road to walk, but if we are to take God's forgiveness of us seriously, we must also forgive Babylon. They, like us, are unworthy, yet they need our forgiveness not our bitterness. Daniel, if you fall into the temptation of biting back, you will not only lessen other people's lives but will find bitterness robs you of your own soul. It will reduce your ability to be happy, your influence to change society and your peace of mind. It will imprison you in a lonely resentment. God has created you for so much more than spiteful living. Please, Daniel, do not yield to the temptation to bite back.

The invitation to be holy

Imagine Daniel, a thousand years from now, if what God did through *your* life is the story told and Nebuchadnezzar is but a footnote. Could a life like that be achieved by blending in or biting back? I don't think so. Significance is birthed in radical conviction. So develop your influence knowing that when God's people are holy, they evoke real history. The rest is just smoke.

Invite Him, not your ego, to sit on the throne of your heart. Let love not bitterness be the ruler of your days. May faithful action not apathetic attitudes define your lifestyle. God is inviting you into a significant life; you must choose to follow. God has created you for holy living. So please, Daniel, don't blend in, don't bite back but accept God's invitation to be holy, and who knows what He will accomplish through your life.

*

I am unsure when I started thinking about asking for the hand of my wife, or even when I began to love her, but I know there was a day when I declared it publicly – a memorable declaration. When I stood among witnesses and we got married, that was a lifelong commitment.

We have discussed about living free in exile but I feel this is the moment to declare your devotion – to decide thoroughly if you are accepting the Lord's invite into this godly adventure. To be one of His people in this foreign land.

It's time.

First, decide in your own heart if you are truly committed.

Then, decide how you can make it public. Create some form of ceremony in which you can declare with clarity your commitment. Your initiative may inspire other believers to do so with you, so include as many as you can in the act. You should take the lead, and open hearts to the Giver of Life.

When this is complete, when you have decided to be an unembarrassed disciple and declared it among friends, you will be ready for the next section of letters.

Keep your eyes open,

Abel

To think about:

1. How do you think Daniel's moving to Babylon is similar to being in a secularising society today?
2. Write down when you have felt the pressure to blend in, the temptation to bite back and the invitation to be holy.
3. Can you remember a moment in your life when you declared your commitment to follow Jesus publicly?

Time to Discus

Therefore everyone who hears these words of mine and puts them into practice is like a wise man who built his house on the rock.

(Matthew 7:24)

I found it hard to write those letters. I kept wanting to mention Jesus by name, I hope you have seen Him foretold as Abel speaks of how God rescues us.

Jesus, in his manifesto sermon – the Sermon on the Mount – calls us to be distinctly different, to be salt and light (Matthew 5:1–16). This change, He says, will happen from the inside out (Matthew 5:17–48). That means to allow this change to occur we need to be real with God, not bluffing our holiness but allowing His presence to become our most defining feature (Matthew 6:1–18). Because it's when we are honest before God that we realise we can really trust Him. It's when we seek first His kingdom and His righteousness that our lives will begin to have real significance and we can join the narrow road that leads to life (Matthew 6:19 – 7:14). Then, as His sermon draws to an end, Jesus says there is real news or fake news, and there are genuine disciples and pretend disciples. You can build your life on a true foundation or a false foundation. And, in closing, Jesus calls us to build our lives on Him, the true foundation for living (Matthew 7:15–27).

In the letters you've just read, Abel is trying to show Daniel the foundation he can build his life upon. He wants to give him some perspective as to the scale of God's kingdom compared to Nebuchadnezzar's. While Abel didn't know Jesus' name yet, allow me to summarise that foundation now, in light of who Jesus is and what He has done.

God creates, rescues and guides. We can see throughout Scripture and in our lives the work of the Trinity at play in God's three main actions. In creation we primarily think of God the Father; in rescue we primarily think of God the Son; in guidance we primarily think of God the Holy Spirit. The foundation of our discipleship as Christians, is that we live in thankful response to what God has done. God creates us in a particular time and a specific place, giving us our fundamental identity, purpose and relationship. Jesus rescues us in grace and truth, inviting us to repent and believe the good news. The Holy Spirit guides us within a commissioned community; we follow, allowing our love-filled lives to spill out as we go and make disciples.

These are the foundations of the path we walk on as Christians. We live as a created, rescued and guided people.

Jesus invites us to build our lives on these foundations.

As Jesus concludes His Sermon on the Mount, it is striking that storms came to both the house built on sand and the house built on rock – both people (Matthew 7:24–27). But Jesus says that when you build your life on His Word, you will have an unsinkable foundation and an unstoppable future. Nothing else can give you that. No matter how skilled you are or how impressive your UCAS form or CV is or even if you're the king of Babylon! The storms of life will still come. When you read the story of Daniel, you will see that difficulties came to both him and the pagan kings he served under, yet, tell me this, whose foundation got rocked?

Storms expose our foundations. Daniel's troubles exposed that he had built his life on the rock-solid foundation of his trust in God. While Babylon was impressive, it was ultimately a house built on sand. When we act like the wise builder and build our lives on Jesus, we have an unsinkable foundation and an unstoppable future.

You see, the Christian has a lot to look forward to, and nothing to fear. That's some starting point to build your life from.

Guide for meeting together

1. Go back over the previous letters and discuss what parts struck you.
2. Take it in turns to pick one of the questions 'to think about' at the end of each letter and share your thoughts.
3. Discuss these questions:
    - What have been some of the 'storms' you have faced in your life? How did they expose your foundations?

- Take in turn each of God's main actions (creating, rescuing and guiding). How can you respond with thankfulness to the God who has created you, rescued you and guides you?
- Abel invited Daniel to commit to God before he read the next set of letters. His next set of letters are about 'how to' live a life that honours God. Are you ready to commit to following Jesus, embracing a lifelong commitment to him?

4. Take some time to consider Jeremiah 6:16: 'This is what the LORD says: "Stand at the crossroads and look; ask for the ancient paths, ask where the good way is, and walk in it, and you will find rest for your souls."' Pray together using the verse as a guide.

Section Three

The Art of Living Free

My eyes will watch over them for their good, and I will bring them back to this land. I will build them up and not tear them down; I will plant them and not uproot them. I will give them a heart to know me, that I am the Lord. They will be my people, and I will be their God, for they will return to me with all their heart.

(Jeremiah 24:6–7)

12

How to Surrender

Like clay in the hand of the potter, so are you in my hand.

(Jeremiah 18:6)

Dear Daniel,

So you've decided yes, you want to be holy! You actually want to do this: to live as a distinct disciple. You want God to be the centre of your attention, the focus of your goals, seated on the throne of your heart.

And it is here, in surrender, where God begins to tell His story through us. It is here where we begin to live fully alive.

When I became a disciple, I really wanted to *do it right*, to 'make it' as a follower – taking notes during temple teaching. When I went for advice, I kept getting the same answer: 'You just got to surrender.' I was frustrated, annoyed even. *Is that it? I thought I had already done that!* Little did I know that faith is no one-night stand but a continual act of giving

God the reins. We are still the same breathing person who knelt yesterday, and we still have the same conditions and responsibilities surrounding us as before. But simply because it's a new day, it's time to hand over the reins again. It's not a giving up but a giving over.

*

Does the clay speak to the potter and ask to become something? Of course not! It's the other way round. The potter sees potential in the clay, lifts it from the pile, throws it on the spinning wheel and begins his work. The clay squelches and squirms under the authority of the master's hands before finally, as it submits to the potter's vision, something is made. I remember this image from a sermon our prophet spoke.

In the hands of a skilled potter, surrendered clay transforms from a worthless lump into something both beautiful and useful. When we surrender to God, He is not clumsy with us but skilfully and carefully crafts us into someone beautiful and useful. We become someone who will both shine for others to see and be useful in the common, daily adventure of audacious faithfulness.

Daniel, you know you are chosen by God – that's not in question. But pride, if left unchecked, can jilt our commitment and restrict our surrender to His will. It must be dealt with. We must kneel each morning in humble acceptance if we are to walk in the fullness of His calling.

Godliness is the art of surrender. To really live we must allow the Potter to reshape us. For He forms us into who we were made to be, making our usefulness more useful and our beauty more beautiful. The daily act of surrender will transform you into a strong, winsome disciple, both showing the better way and living it.

God is interested in the details of our lives. The way we speak, the way we shop, the responsibilities we hold and the way we hold them all matter to God. The actions of a disciple are not automatically godly because of his conversion but because of his surrendered obedience.

The Lord is shaping you for a significant purpose that will shine brightly in the darkness of Babylon. Great moments will come, but your usefulness and how bright you shine will be built on the daily discipline of surrender. To surrender properly you must know two things: your life matters and God has a better vision.

Your life matters

You are not some accident. A loving God created you. You are not – as our pagan entrepreneurs would say – 'trying to make something of yourself'. *God* has made you to tell a unique story. So walk in that, be you, but not the *you* of your selfish rebellion. Be who God envisioned when He made you, when He rescued you and when He set you in the mix of this new culture, where you can live whole and bright among the broken darkness.

God has a better vision

Pottery is messy work. A potter's hands are mucked with clay, feeling every impurity and air pocket as they work the wheel. But their eyes see further than what the clay is; they also see ahead to what the clay can be. Yes, a potter's hands are mucked with clay, but their eyes are clear with vision.

Disciples, like pots, are made up-close. We must invite God's hands to work in the very hour by hour of our living. It's during morning prayers and preparing meals, while we love our neighbour and be known by our brothers and sisters, that God's purposes really find their way to changing our hearts. For our God sees beyond who we are to who we can be and invites us to change.

Yet while God is interested in the everydayness of our every day, His vision is not only local. The One who holds us in His hands also holds the stars. He is ruling the world, raising kings and forming nations.

We must keep both these visions in perspective: that the God who is calling the nations to Himself is interested in the details of how we live our lives; that the God who created the universe is also interested in how we speak to our neighbours. From here I can draw only one conclusion: that God sees our everyday acts not as superfluous to world change but as the centre stage of His unfolding plans. He believes our actions are not consequential but weapons; torches that can light up the darkness; beacons that can show the world the way home.

*

There is a temptation, more acute for you in exile, to reduce our participation in the world to a small corner. It is easy to think our lives can only do small things, to just fold our arms and wait for the exile to be over. But a mature faith knows that while God is involved in the mucky art of untwisting our lives, He also has a reason for this exile and a better vision for the world. He is moulding you to play your part in that vision.

Try to grow an olive tree in a small jar and it won't work. You will get a tiny shoot, but an olive tree was not created for a tiny existence. So too, if we try to be godly with only a small vision of the world, we will never grow towards making a real difference. An olive tree with space, good soil and sunlight will stretch into the sky, creating homes for wildlife, shade for the weary as well as olives, of course! So too, when you live knowing your life matters and planting that intentionality into the soil of God's vision, will you stretch into the sky. Your influence will grow steady and strong, providing hope for the weary and inspiring faithfulness in the young.

You have been uprooted from Jerusalem to Babylon, and must now plant your roots in this strange and brilliant country. So, Daniel, keep your soil enriched with the Scriptures, keep your branches strong with virtues, keep your vision open to the possibilities of heaven.

Keep your eyes open,

Abel

PS Surrendering grows mature with frequency. The more mature a disciple is, the more frequent is their surrender. To start you off, let me suggest you submit each morning. Open your hands before God and say these words: 'God, I am Yours, all Yours. You can do whatever You want with my life.'

Then step into your day, which is what our next letter will be about.

To think about:

1. Read and think through Jeremiah 18:1–12. How do the people of Judah respond to God's invitation to reform their lives like a potter does with a pot?
2. What can help you remember that your life matters and that God has a better vision?
3. How can you incorporate the daily act of surrender into your morning routine?

13

How to Live Each Day

I will give them a heart to know me.
(Jeremiah 24:7)

Dear Daniel,

After a few years of trying to find my way, I met Eli. You met him once, just after you started to talk. You would have loved him. Your father allowed me to visit him each week after my conversion. Eli taught me the flow of the Torah. He demonstrated how each page is liveable. He showed me how the Scriptures simplify our lives, freeing us with an unsinkable foundation and giving us the hope of an unstoppable future.

Most of what I have shared over these letters began as a conversation with him. That's the nature of discipleship – it can't be bought or sucked out of the clouds. Disciples are made up-close, remember? Our faith is local, it's dusty and it's worked out in the normality of everyday life.

*

We only have one word in our language to denote both 'work' and 'worship': *avoda.* Neither Eli nor I believe this to be accidental but a profound introduction into how to view our days. God plants us in a large space and calls us to worship. We are to work, not just from the shoulders down but to worship with our intellect, our skillset and our ambitions. God invites our imagination, our entrepreneurial spirit and our decision-making into this adoring partnership.

Many find their identity solely in what they do. Others believe they can be themselves without doing anything. Both are wrong. Whether we realise it or not, our daily activities are acts of adoration; we toil for someone or something. It's hard for me to imagine what your labour in Babylon will involve, but I know it will not be separate from your worship – they are one and the same. So let's consider how we live each day.

A day

If you enter your day with a schedule, *time* becomes the important commodity. You'll negotiate what is worth your time and what isn't. You'll begin to swap out things because you *haven't got the time.* In effect, you'll be less free. With time as the governing factor, responsibilities will become chores, relationships will become free-time activities and rest will become optional. Even your friendship with God will inevitably become something you 'have to do' within the time you have, and therefore something you can swap out if time demands it. This is how I viewed my days before Eli gave me a new perspective, which has since become my practice.

Instead of entering your day with a schedule, enter it as an act of worship. *God*, not time, will become your governing focus. Included in your worship will be all that you have to do that day, but you'll be doing them to God. Indeed, you'll be doing them for God. Viewing your day as an act of worship enables your whole life to be in constant connection. Your relationship with God is no longer a time-slotted duty on your schedule; it's an ongoing reality.

Achieving this will require a mindset and a practice.

A mindset

Be with God in every moment, in the ordinary. Cultivate an ongoing awareness of His presence. Carry this connection into every room you enter, every mountain you climb, every place you lay your head. Make the shift from distraction to devotion, from chaos to simplicity. Living each moment with God will bring clarity to your mind. Rather than moving in many directions, you'll move in one direction. The world tries to do many things at the same time – it's exhausting. Disciples do many things in a row, as an act of worship – it's that simple (though not easy!).

A practice

Yes, be with God in every moment, but also create moments to be with God. Any relationship is like this. In marriage you 'do life together', but you also pause life so that you can 'be together'. Being aware of God's presence is sweet, but it is sweeter still to stop what you are doing, walk somewhere and be still with your God.

My suggestion is to stop working for a short while three times a day. Open your windows towards home, kneel, be quiet and wait. When your attention is no longer on your tasks or your needs, start talking and keep listening, expectant for what God will say. This practice will keep you mindful of His presence throughout the day, keeping you alert and attentive to His guidance.

Keep your eyes open,

Abel

To think about:

1. It takes bravery to live your days as acts of worship. Read Daniel 6, then consider how the themes of worship, daily practice, bravery and witness all play a part in this famous story.
2. How can you cultivate a mindset of worship in your every day?
3. How can you develop a practice of prayer in your every day?

14

How to Change the World

The Lord will create a new thing on earth.
(Jeremiah 31:22)

Dear Daniel,

Hope is no vain condition of the heart. Hope is what we know will happen, based on a real God who acted in our own history and calls us each day to follow. Every morning, we hope, and each evening we can say God is still faithful. For we who have great reason to believe, hope is reliance on God's Word.

Acting on the Word of God is the most practical thing you can do, even if it seems idiotic to those around you. Noah was considered a fool for building his ark until it rained; you may be considered a fool until God's Word to us is fulfilled. Allowing what you believe to decide how you act is living with hopeful practicality. We can live our lives with the freedom and gumption to act boldly for our

God, undeterred by the expected edict of society. Being courageous is being hope-determined. Being authentic is allowing what you believe to influence your actions.

Noah, Abraham, Joseph, Moses, Joshua and Jeremiah did not allow their current reality to dictate their actions, but acted on the Word of God. Even when present evidence pointed against their decisions (building a boat; leaving Ur; collecting grain; confronting Pharaoh; placing both feet in the Jordan; buying a field in desolated Judah), they acted on the Word of God. Each act was a contradiction to their reality, but each act was a response to the hope they professed, and each time God created a way.

So here's to those who build boats in the desert, are knee-deep in the River Jordan waiting for God to act and are buying fields while under siege. Here's to the determined hopeful who are practical with God's promises – who act on what they hope for and who live in authenticity to the faith they hold.

*

Your ability to show the world the one true God will no longer come from any authority, sway or power you have. All has been reset. You have been placed in the seat of insignificance, so God's Word will only shine from your integrity and faith's practice in your life. Authenticity not authority is the frontline of God's kingdom in Babylon.

I imagine you will have to model God's kingdom before you can advocate for it. Your honest life lived openly, unembarrassed and generous with the values of the Torah, will shine all the brighter against the backdrop of a self-centred culture hell-bent on finding success. If Samson were with you, I'm sure he'd grab a jawbone and fight his way through! However, this is not the time for such things. Instead of using a jawbone, use your example.

There are those who will take the position of the warrior and 'bite back', as we've looked at before. But we are to seek peace, dwell in the land and bless the nations. We are not warriors with swords and spears, but rather with wisdom. We are wisdom warriors, making the correct decisions on how we live by knowing the real story of who is in charge. A display of God's kingdom will be our most effective weapon in seeing His kingdom come.

'Be true to yourself' can mean too many things. It's advice from someone with more tongue than truth. I would rather tell you to be true to God's promises, His ways and the commission He has given you. Be real. Don't pray lies or try to bluff God. Faking it won't cut it. Being honest with yourself and being true to God is the recipe for authentic faith.

Do you remember the Rekabites? The descendants of Jehonadab, son of Rekab? They were commanded, 'Neither you nor your descendants must ever drink wine. Also you must never build houses, sow seed or plant vineyards' (Jeremiah 35:6–7). Like us they are a people called to a unique existence, yet God asked Jeremiah to invite them for a wine party in the temple! I mean, why would God do that? Surely to teach us the capacity to live in a culture while remaining authentic to who you are – Jeremiah's wine stayed in the bowls. The Rekabites lived out for us the possibility of maintaining a true identity and a disciplined distinctiveness in a foreign land.

They were a commanded people. And while we have commands, we are, at our core, a commissioned people. A commissioned community to be priests to the nations, a light to the world, showing who God is and what a life with Him looks like.

Daniel, you are secure. God is on your side and His grace is enough for you. So go for it. If you get the opportunity to shape medical practice in Babylon, get involved. If you get the chance to form a community of believers, do it. If there's a moment to speak with the king, take it. If there's an opening to be part of the justice system, jump in. If you get the chance to help Nebuchadnezzar rule his kingdom, do it. But do not do it as a Babylonian – do it as a disciple. For there is nothing more powerful in God's hands than someone with an authentic faith who engages in their society. That's how to change the world.

Keep your eyes open,

Abel

To think about:

1. You'll find this intriguing story about the Rekabites in Jeremiah 35. God uses it to teach the Israelites about faithfulness. Abel uses the story to invite Daniel to be faithful to his commission as an ambassador of the kingdom of God. What does it look like in your life to 'maintain a true identity and a disciplined distinctiveness in a foreign land'?
2. What does engaging with your society, as a Christian, look like for you?

15

How to Doubt

Yet my people have forgotten me ...
which made them stumble in their ways,
in the ancient paths.

(Jeremiah 18:15)

Dear Daniel,

What do we do when we doubt if God's ways are best?

Doubts never come from reason but by seeing. They come through observing something that clashes with the Word of God. Even though you *know* the reality, you still take a second look, see the contradiction and begin to doubt. With all you will see over the coming years, I would expect doubts to come. And rather than running from them or trying to push them into the unconscious part of your mind, I would embrace them. Work through them to become a stronger, more culturally aware disciple.

The first psalm of Asaph (Psalm 73) tells of someone

who doubts, nearly losing their foothold on the ancient paths, but as the psalm closes, we see a renewed enthusiasm to follow the God who knows best. We spent some time reciting it a couple of years back, if you remember. Today, I want to show you how, when we are unsure if God's ways are best, this psalm can guide us through the doubt into a stronger trust in God.

*

To begin dealing with doubt, your first step is to voice the truth that jars with what you're witnessing. Say it clear and short. Just as Asaph starts by voicing his conviction:

> *Surely God is good to Israel,*
> *to those who are pure in heart.*
>
> *(Psalm 73:1)*

Then you can begin to tell God what you are seeing and how it doesn't match what you believe. For Asaph, it was evil people getting away scot-free (outlined in verses 4–12). For you, it may be something else. Being honest here is key: what is it that does not match up? How is this a betrayal? Is God being who He said He would be?

Once you've asked those questions straight, and there is nothing more to add, the psalm takes us back to a firm footing on the ancient paths. We're invited to do three things: to go to the sanctuary, to compare paths and to reach for His hand.

Step 1: Go to the sanctuary

As I've already said, the doubt doesn't come from reason or experience, but by *seeing* something. If we were to compare our faith with Babylonian religion purely on the grounds of reason, we would knock it dead. Our faith makes sense. Babylon doesn't even know what it believes, never mind being able to articulate it in the first place. But as doubt comes from seeing and not reasoning, there we must give Babylon the upper hand, because it certainly *looks* like they are doing better than us. Babylon is thriving and we are in ruins.

You may, then, understandably become envious of those who flaunt their pride before God. Your first port of call, Asaph tell us, is to enter the sanctuary. Join with others who are worshipping. You will not have the temple in Babylon, but that matters little: the key is to worship with others and remind your senses who God is. Like Asaph says, 'When I tried to understand all this, it troubled me deeply till I entered the sanctuary of God' (verses 16–17).

When your eyes are conflicted, reawaken your senses to the work of God in your life. Sing and fellowship. Pray and fast. When that is done, you are ready to doubt the doubt with reason, and that's the next step.

Step 2: Compare paths

Now it's time to consider what life would be like if you did step off the path of discipleship and into a pagan lifestyle. Write it down on two sides of a page – the pros and cons of going your own way versus living with God. Comparison gives clarity and it won't take long to realise which path is the 'slippery ground'.

A child walking beside the wrong legs looks up in horror when they see an untrusted stranger guiding their steps rather than their father. It is when we actually compare paths – the righteous with the unrighteous – that we gain disdain for the lifestyle we just flirted with. And we grow a fresh love for the God of heaven who sings over us with rejoicing as He plans our steps. As Asaph says, 'Surely you place *them* on slippery ground' (verse 18, my emphasis).

Step 3: Reach for His hand

Finally, we are back in the place of trust. We are aware of God's presence, we have compared the way of the world to the way of God, and now we're ready to entrust ourselves to Him afresh. It is time to reach up and wait, to wait for God to take our hand and lead us on. This waiting requires vulnerability. But in reaching for His hand we find not the pain of punishment but the presence of a parent, longing to guide us in a generous life. So, like Asaph, we can then conclude:

Yet I am always with you;
you hold me by my right hand.
You guide me with your counsel,
and afterwards you will take me into glory.
Whom have I in heaven but you?

And earth has nothing I desire besides you.
My flesh and my heart may fail,
but God is the strength of my heart
and my portion for ever.

(Psalm 73:23–26)

Keep your eyes open,

Abel

To think about:

1. Have you had moments of doubt? Did you see them as an enemy of your faith or as something which would eventually help?
2. Read Psalm 73. What do you notice about the journey the psalm takes you on?
3. Are you doubting something now? What is it and can you use this psalm to work it through?

16

How to Pray for Resilience

They will be like a tree planted by the water
that sends out its roots by the stream …
and never fails to bear fruit.

(Jeremiah 17:8)

Dear Daniel,

I wait with weight tonight, but even here I know there is a God who wants to listen to me. A child who is being denied their mother's milk will cling to their mother, finding comfort in the very person who is refusing them the thing they long for. Our God, who has ordained the destruction and exile I'm witnessing … is still the One to whom I cling.

I long to be with you, but this is not God's will. God has denied me such a sweet end to my life. Yet I'll cling to Him still, for I know He is the source of all comfort, the writer of our stories. Besides, who else is there? Where else can I go? He is our *only* hope. To Him, I direct my prayers. I pray for resilience.

I wouldn't let the Levites hear me say this but I don't think you can get *better* at prayer. It's the wrong way to think about it. We don't become better – we are either honest before God or we are lying. Naked or masked. Real or fake. We do not study God as a subject or an idea, to figure out the best way to work Him onto our side. God *is* on our side and prayer is the act of coming before Him, to be His.

Prayer is real because God is real – not because you say the right words.

Prayer works because God is at work – not because you have a magic formula to get Him on your side.

Eli once gave me six prayers that would develop resilience in my faith. Today, I want to offer six prayers to you. These should not become your exact prayers. Rather, think of these as titles for prayers to pray in exile, to help build the resilience you'll need. To help you be a lifelong follower.

1. 'It's just me'

Honesty is the first step to develop any relationship. There is no point trying to bluff God. We need to be open with God, presenting ourselves as we are, knowing God loves us too much to leave us as we are.

Praying, 'It's just me – this is who I am right now' is the level of honesty needed for this relationship to flourish. It opens us up to be changed by a God who knows better and it is a great starting place for the adventure of faith.

2. 'Strengthen my muscles'

You can't catch fish with a lump of coal and you can't make wise decisions without Scripture. As you seek to live as a child of God in an unwholesome culture, you will need to develop muscles of discernment. You'll need to know three key things if you want to live a holy life in exile: you must know the way of God inside out; you must become skilled at knowing your own tendencies; and you must be able to recognise the directional pull of Babylon.

Praying, 'Strengthen my muscles' puts you in the learner position. You are the first generation of disciples to live through this age, and with that scale of change happening around you. Remaining teachable with the Scriptures open – an ear to heaven with your feet on earth – is the right approach for developing godly discernment.

3. 'Ground my ambitions'

You will have access to a whole new world. This will expose two traps. You could become a glutton for distraction and be lazy in your ambitions. Alternatively, you could fake yourself into thinking you are successful when your attempts do not even involve the core principles of our faith. As a disciple, you will need to ground yourself with the central instructions of God. Rather than chasing dead-end dreams or becoming distracted from your purpose, become aware of your giftings and dream big within the purposes of God.

Praying, 'Ground my ambitions' plants your dreams in faithfulness, enabling you to live a high-achieving life.

Embrace a life of intentionality and change the world. but do it from the baseline of your love for God, your neighbour and this world.

4. 'Give me mentors'

You cannot disciple yourself. I hope these letters are useful, but they are no substitute for someone who will walk with you. Discipleship is personal but not individual. You will need the wisdom of wrinkles and the power of true friendship if you are to discern the way ahead.

'Give me mentors' is the prayer of a humble disciple. And because relationships change and move, you should pray this at the start of each new season. I have tears as I write this one, as I can no longer be your mentor. So, Daniel, it is time to pray this afresh. May your next mentor see in you what I see.

5. 'Heal my wounds'

Grief is valid. Being positive will not cut it. Looking for silver linings is like noticing a rainbow as you fall off a cliff. Life isn't always an upward curve – people suffer, so learn to lament. When Josiah heard the book of Moses, he tore his clothes – it was time to lament what had gone wrong, to heal, to change. When Jehoiakim heard the message, he tore the scroll – unwilling to change, he tried to make everything look alive when the core was rotten. This is when Jeremiah thought fit to begin reciting his acrostic poems, a comprehensive voicing of our pain. Lamentations for our nation, empowering us to grieve, validating our sadness. Sincerely, I hope he will write them down, because no doubt history will repeat itself, pain will revisit God's people and we will again need a guide to articulate our prayers.

'Heal my wounds' is the prayer of someone who knows they need God. Our nation will fail again, we will fail again and we must not cover the rotten apple with a new skin. Learn to bring your wounds to God, and God will be there ready to forgive, ready to heal. When you fail, pray in the company of Jeremiah and act with the character of Josiah.

6. 'I'm all Yours'

The knees of a godly person look like camel's knees – they've become swollen from kneeling so often. Babylon doesn't need more skilled people, strong people or smart people; Babylon needs surrendered people, who can live in the depths of the city serving a higher throne.

Praying, 'I'm all yours' acknowledges how doing anything for God must start in surrender. So that is where you begin each day, on your knees dedicating yourself to the Ancient of Days.

That's all six ... Use them.

But I have one more suggestion. If you want to prepare yourself for a lifetime of following, learn to pray the psalms. They are like the collection of stars above us. At first glance you can see that they dazzle, and you can make out a few popular shapes. Yet as you gaze longer, you see that they dazzle all the more. Indeed, look hard and long, for years and years, and you will begin to see more than just dots in the sky but a universe shining light on your own experience.

The psalmists are tour guides of the heart, giving us bravery to be honest before God, to be direct and unclichéd. They give us the skills we need to work on our prayers, so they become portraits of our inner selves – open before the God of heaven.

Can you live a full life for the glory of God in exile? If I had a hundred hearts, I'd believe it with each one. Like the tree that 'sends out its roots by the stream' (Jeremiah 17:8), grow your roots in God's direction and you will be not only resilient but fruitful.

Keep your eyes open,

Abel

To think about:

1. Circle one of Abel's six prayers that is of particular importance for you.
2. How could you use these prayers to develop your own prayer life?

17

How to Make Decisions

Where is the word of the L*ORD*?

(Jeremiah 17:15)

Dear Daniel,

I'll try and keep this letter brief as I must take a trip tonight to get more paper, ink and food. The city has had a noisy week, but seems quieter today. I've been writing in the olive press with my candles for a while now, going outside only before dawn for prayer with your father.

*

Faith in the past should be celebrated, but faith is not lived in the past. It is always present, always now: this decision; this opportunity; this community; this person. Now, what will you do today?

God will always be with you. However, there will be constant decisions to make on your end. Often God invites us to a role and leaves the specifics to us. When you have to make a decision and the options are not clear, you can get confused. I find these two things help to simplify: developing non-negotiables and having a framework for thinking through decisions.

Developing non-negotiables

Before you buy a field, you need to know how much you have to spend. Before making decisions, you need to know what is not on the negotiation table. There is a simplicity here that's helpful in discernment, a first step in developing the muscles you will need to negotiate the times you are in. The Rekabites displayed this ability well.

Those things that you know are fundamental to your God-given identity and purpose are not open for discussion. For example, one of mine is that I will pray with your father each morning. Others involve my responsibility to my sister and towards you, along with some clear principles central to being a disciple.

Your list of non-negotiables can be yeses or noes, including things you will never do, always do or responsibilities you will put first. To think these will 'just happen' is flippant. If you want to be a loyal friend, plan to be one. Make a list at the start of each new season outlining who you will absolutely be. This is a great first step.

A framework for thinking through decisions

When you are faced with something and need to act, think

of the first three letters in your name: D (decline?). A (accept?). N (negotiate?). These three words are helpful as a starting place. If you are expected to do something in Babylon, you can think to yourself:

- Is this something I should *decline*?
- Is this something I should *accept*?
- Is this something I should *negotiate*?

A few examples ...

While you'll always want to work things through amicably, if you are asked to do something that is outright opposed to your faith – to stop praying, to enjoy a prostitute, to bow to a foreign god – this is something you should *decline*. Do it in a clear, calm manner. It's wrong, so decline it!

If you are invited to learn about Babylonian culture, this is something you can *accept*. It is important to learn about where you are, and it doesn't contradict the core principles of your faith. It's good, so accept it!

If you are expected to dine at a gathering linked to pagan worship, this is something you can *negotiate*. It is key to note the invite. The person who invited you is being kind and has unintentionally given you this conundrum. It is a good opportunity, yet crosses a line fundamental to your faith. So accept the invite but advise why you can't eat that particular food or do that particular ritual. It's redeemable – there is a way you can honour both your host and God – so negotiate!

You can start to think through some other scenarios now, even as you read this letter. And be as specific as you can ... What about your name? I hear that Nebuchadnezzar's custom is to change his subjects' names as an attempt to reinvent them as devoted citizens. So will you call yourself by the name they give you? Are you going to decline the name change, accept it or negotiate?

Even if you do change your name, please remember the first three letters of Daniel! We don't have to be caught in insecurity and caution; we have the freedom to train our discernment muscles so we can make decisions and live holy, high-achieving lives. And the reason I'm reminding you of your name is so you will remember what it means: God is my judge.

*

No-one wakes and thinks, 'Today, I want to make choices I'll regret,' but we often do, almost always unthinkingly. Decisions are important, too important to assume that you can just follow your heart. The heart wants what is right but it has a crafty guide who disguises the light for darkness, who fogs our ability to see the briers and identify the demons. So we need help with our decisions. The first step is to decide to be decisive, to take your life seriously enough, to have a considered prayerfulness with the choices that lie ahead. Then the methods above will be useful. But ultimately remember you serve a God who guides. Don't just keep your eyes open; keep your *ears* open! He *will* guide. You only have to follow.

Keep your eyes open,

Abel

PS Oh, one last thing – what do you do if you've made a wrong choice and find yourself far along the path of regret? Well, don't cling to a mistake just because you've spent a long time making it. Make amends and start afresh.

To think about:

1. Underline a sentence from this letter that you could take as advice for your own life.
2. Can you find examples of Daniel declining, accepting and negotiating in Babylon throughout Daniel chapters 1–6?
3. What decisions are you making at the moment?
4. What would be on your list of non-negotiables?

18

A Note from Your Father

Daniel,

It's your father.

Abel has died.

We found him face down by the river. I don't know what happened, but his head is bruised. He must have been on his way back from getting more writing supplies – we found paper and a new quill, as well as some mucked flatbread nearby. The last of the invaders are still with us and he would have looked suspicious – a well-dressed man at night carrying paper. Either that or he met someone desperate enough to kill for the food.

Daniel, I am so sorry. I am sorry for everything. I pray it was the right decision to let you go instead of hiding you. May God have mercy on me be it wrong.

I placed a family ring on Abel's finger before we buried him in the west garden. He was one of us, loyal to you, to the end.

I'm in his makeshift writing hut here – the olive press. There is a table with a lamp and notes on scraps of paper lying around, then one neat pile of new parchment. On top was a note for me: 'Letters for Daniel', followed by instructions for this very circumstance. It's like he had made peace knowing any day could be his last. He signs off with a simple statement: 'Thanks for sharing your son with me.'

Abel loved you, Daniel. And I know you loved him. Love seems to have a way of multiplying; the more you give, the more you have. I've been reading through his letters and wondering how I could tell you this news, or if I should just send them as they are. But he sacrificed everything to give you this final mentoring, so I am writing to let you know.

Among the scrap paper is one numbered 18. I assume it is the outline for his next letter to you. Maybe he planned to write another few; maybe he planned to keep writing until he was found – who knows? I will include it next. Though it is just his outline, you can see his headings and initial thoughts. Even here, you can see his heart for you.

I'm so glad he thought us friends. To me, he was a brother. He always kept that servant edict though. I will mourn him deeply. While I thanked him many times before the invasion, I regret I never fully thanked him for writing these letters to you. Heaven knows the difference they will make.

I can't help but wonder why he always signed off, 'Keep your eyes open.' It puzzles me. I never heard him say it before. Yet as I continue to read, I think he's suggesting it become a moto.

Keep your eyes open: become attentive to what is happening around you; pay attention to the way God is working so you can join in. That's the key. I gave you the name Daniel because I had a vision of a man who would live with honour before God as his judge. So focus on God, then keep a careful eye on yourself and the people around you. Keep your eyes open – I believe this is trustworthy council.

*

I do have one nugget to add to all the advice and perspectives Abel has laid out for you.

Find good people, Daniel. Find friends you can be honest with, and be the first one in the group to be vulnerable. Good friends make life enjoyable, help you laugh and give you more guidance than you realise. When the blanket of darkness swallows your life, you will hear them singing the next verse of your own song. Their hope will give you hope, their faith will give you faith, their strength will give you strength and their love will soften your heart to grow more love.

People are never the enemy, so treat your captors as people too. They are made in the image of God, longing to be known and loved – just like everyone else. Maybe in time they too will be counted among your friends.

I love you Daniel. Pray also for me.

I'll see you on the eternal shore.

Until then – live free.

19

How to Dream Again

Abel's initial notes for another letter to Daniel

The Lord *appeared to us in the past, saying:*

'I have loved you with an everlasting love;
I have drawn you with unfailing kindness.'
(Jeremiah 31:3)

When I was young, my generation had the excitement of revival under Josiah. We hoped it would propel us forward as a nation but we've been sorely disappointed. Our nation is now in ruins.

For you exiles, it's time to dream again, to capture the vision of God in a new way and dream about what your lives could become.

How can these dreams begin?
Know your gifts – ask yourself: what do you think God is

asking you to do? Then use these three 'P's to get there:

- Priorities – what do you want to achieve with your life?
- Principles – what values should ground your ambitions?
- Possibilities – where can you begin?

What about when you fail?

When you fail and are stuck in a hole, fill the hole with the hard lessons you have learned, use it as a foundation. Then join the Revealer of Mysteries in dreaming a bigger dream.

Daniel, you are free to dream because you are free from fear. Remember, we are in a story with a promise, we have great reason to believe. We are partners with the great Manager of the Heavens. As our prophet says:

'The days are coming,' declares the Lord,
'when I will raise up for David a righteous Branch,
a King who will reign wisely
and do what is just and right in the land.
In his days Judah will be saved
and Israel will live in safety.
This is the name by which he will be called:
The Lord Our Righteous Saviour.

(Jeremiah 23:5–6)

To think about:

1. If Daniel were to write a tribute for Abel, what would he say?
2. Abel notes, 'It's time to dream again.' Spend time considering: what dreams does God have for your life?
3. Are you ready to dream a bigger dream for your life?

Time to Discuss

As a prisoner for the Lord, then, I urge you to live a life worthy of the calling you have received.

(Ephesians 4:1)

Well done, you've made it! I don't know how much you connected with Abel as you've read his letters, but for years now I've been watching courageous young people live out their faith in a world full of distractions, distant from truth. I have wondered, all this time, what advice a mentor of Daniel's would have given him. How he would have prepared Daniel to live out his faith within the Babylonian empire. I wish I could go back in time and interview Abel and Daniel or have them as guests on a podcast! Sadly, it's not possible. This is our time, not theirs. Yet I hope their story can shed light on our way ahead. I hope it can embolden us and give us wisdom in how we can live for Jesus, robustly and freely, in our secularising world.This has been my best attempt at thinking through the discipleship Daniel might have received. I hope these letters have sparked your imagination, taken you to the place of faith, raised your hands to reach for guidance and opened your lips to sing His praise.

In the very first letter Abel says, 'Imagine coming to the end of your life and realising you've lived the wrong story.' Can you imagine what that would feel like?

My friend Clodagh has been one of the courageous

young people I've watched live out their faith in this cultural moment. She is now one of my colleagues and spends her days quoting John 10:10. She tells every young person she talks to, 'Jesus is always better. You are never missing out when you choose to follow Him.' And maybe sadder than the regret of realising you've lived the wrong story would be to know the right way and still not live it – to know Jesus is better and still not give Him your all.

Imagine choosing to build your life on the sandy ground of the world when there is a sure foundation ready to build from. How foolish. Abel has delt with some of the questions he thinks Daniel will face, given him the foundations of the paths he is to walk on as a disciple, and now invites Daniel to start building. Each letter in the section you've just read is a how-to. Abel doesn't want Daniel simply to know the truth, but to live it. To live the high-achieving life of faithfulness we see documented in the Bible. So Abel gets practical with Daniel before tragedy strikes.

Paul, in his letter to the Ephesians, has a similar request. He urges us to 'live a life worthy of the calling you have received' (Ephesians 4:1). It is the pivotal verse of the book. In chapters 1–3 he spends his time outlining the 'calling you have received', then he invites us to 'live a life worthy' of that calling. Chapters 1–3 are invitational, telling us of the complete work of Jesus and that we can come to Him and be welcomed into His family. Chapters 4–6 are instructional, showing us that being a Christian is no anti-climax, that we can live out this life in all its fullness.

I wonder how many young 'Daniels' are reading this now, wondering if they can really live a life worthy of the calling they have received. The answer is clear: God not only calls us to believe but invites us to follow. To step out in faith knowing that the Ancient of Days is with us every step of the way.

Maybe you've heard the children's song 'Dare to be a Daniel'. Well, I could dare you to be that but I'd rather dare you to follow Jesus with all you've got. He is worth it all.

Guide for meeting together

1. Go back over the previous letters and discuss what parts struck you.
2. Take it in turns to pick one of the questions 'to think about' at the end of each letter and share your thoughts.
3. Discuss these questions:
   - How did you feel when you heard Abel had died?
   - Which of the letters contained advice you really needed to hear?
   - What advice do you think God is giving you as you enter the next season of life?
   - What are the one or two things you want to remember as you finish reading this book?
4. Pray together as you bring your time to an end.

You may have guessed that I enjoy letters! Feel free to reach out. I'd love to hear from anyone who's read this book. My email address is: andy@exodusonline.org.uk

Epilogue

> *It is for freedom that Christ has set us free. Stand firm, then.*
>
> ***(Galatians 5:1)***

This series of letters was originally put together to help two young men I am mentoring deal with the changes they faced as they moved away from home for university.

Adam and Jack's giftedness reminds me of Daniel, whose faithfulness sparked this project. They went to university in September 2020, mid-pandemic, leaving home to isolate in a student room as they studied via Zoom links. A strange start to the university experience.

I would send them a couple of letters in the post and then we would video call at the weekend to discuss. At first I was going to write letters straight to them – 'Dear Adam' and 'Dear Jack'. But since the example of Daniel had been in my imagination for some ten years and I saw his capability in these two young men, I chose a different approach. I decided to study the history, embrace the teaching of the time and prove that the story of the Babylonian exile is indeed relevant to what young people are facing today. So I dived deeper and created Abel. Then the three of us would see what we could gain from observing Abel's letters and how he prepared Daniel for his significant life. These letters ignited conversations that proved fruitful in helping us follow Jesus in our modern-day exile.

My first letter to Adam and Jack was clumsy, a bit too serious and about twice the length it needed to be! But that mattered less than the intention behind it: to stand with these two young disciples as they lived for Jesus in an unfamiliar environment. In closing, I offer you a challenge – who can you write to? I'm sure you'll do a better job than me. And I'm sure it'll make the world of difference.

Acknowledgements

While there are no direct quotes, much has been informed by the work of brilliant thinkers to whom I'm indebted:

The late Eugene Peterson was a fantastic writer; his books are like a cool drink for the tired Christian – I have been refreshed many times. The framework for the baseline discipleship letters (created, rescued and guided) was inspired by Peterson's spiritual theology series. The first of the five-book series, *Christ Plays in Ten Thousand Places* (Hodder & Stoughton, 2008), is split into three sections: creation, history and community, to give a Trinitarian, biblically whole, Christ-centred base for discipleship. Also, where I write in letter 11 about the pot being 'something both useful and beautiful', this is a concept picked up from Peterson's remarkable book on Jeremiah: *Run with the Horses* (IVP, 2019).

I wholeheartedly recommend his writing to you. *A Long Obedience in the Same Direction* (IVP, 2021), *Leap over the Wall* (HarperSanFrancisco, 2002) or the books mentioned above are a great place to start.

Daniel Smith-Christopher outlines the concept of

'wisdom warrior' in his book *A Biblical Theology of Exile* (Fortress Press, 2022). This concept was made real to me through BibleProject's video 'The Way of the Exile'. You can see all BibleProject's videos, blogs and podcasts at www.bibleproject.com

The teaching of Desi Maxwell has so enthused my vision for Jesus and my understanding of the Hebrew Scriptures. The wild horses of the Negev illustration in letter 7 came through a phone call with Desi discussing this project. I first studied under Desi at Belfast Bible College and have engaged with his content online since. Check out www.xplorations.org for more.

Rick Hill's friendship and leading is a well of inspiration. The concept of remembering in the darkness what you learn in the light came from a talk he gave. He has recently written a book: *Deep Roots of Resilient Disciples* (Timeless Publications, 2021).

Peter Lynas from the Evangelical Alliance UK often teaches on the nature of being created in God's image. It is from him I learned the significance of Genesis 1 and 2 in seeing our fundamental identity, purpose and relationships as God-given. You'll find Peter here: www.eauk.org

Timothy Keller is a grounded Bible teacher. Abel's teaching on Psalm 73 in chapter 15 is inspired by a sermon of his I once heard. Find more at www.timothykeller.com

Patton Taylor, Principal Emeritus at Union Theological College, was an informed friend throughout this project, his expertise and guidance much appreciated.

Chris Agnew and Clodagh Dickson have been faithful encouragers throughout.

Debbie, thanks for believing in me, always. And to our children: I pray you will learn to stand on grace and live with compassion in your eyes, a song in your mouth and boldness in your steps.

Finally, I would like to acknowledge my own mentors:

Norman McCorkell

Lynda and the late Norman Lynas

Jim Brown

Jose Cummings

Knox Jones

Ricky Ferguson

Mum and Dad

– thanks for making the world of difference in my life.

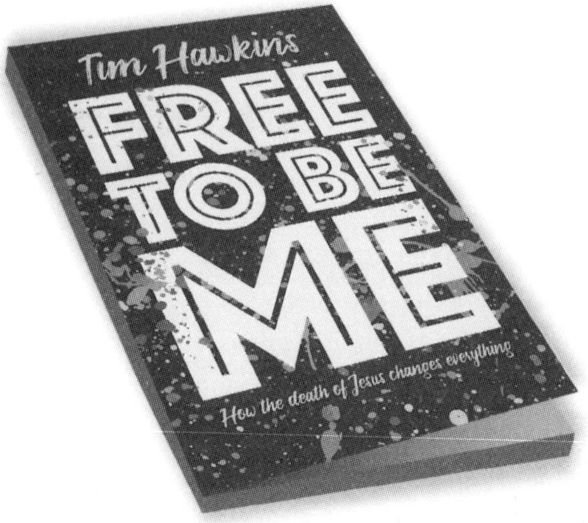

Tim Hawkins
FREE TO BE ME
How the death of Jesus changes everything